Cesare Beccaria

The Genius of *On Crimes and Punishments*

John Hostettler

Cesare Beccaria
The Genius of *On Crimes and Punishments*
John Hostettler

ISBN 9781904380 634 (Paperback)
ISBN 9781906534 936 (e-book)

Published 2011 by
Waterside Press Ltd.
Sherfield Gables
Sherfield on Loddon
Hook
Hampshire
United Kingdon RG27 0JG

Telephone
+44(0)1256 882250
Low cost UK landline calls
0845 2300 733
E-mail
enquiries@watersidepress.co.uk
Online catalogue
WatersidePress.co.uk

Copyright
© 2010 This work is the copyright of John Hostettler. All intellectual property and associated rights are hereby asserted and reserved by the author in full compliance with UK, European and international law. No part of this book may be copied, reproduced, stored in any retrieval system or transmitted in any form or by any means, including in hard copy or on the internet, without the prior written permission of the publishers to whom all such rights have been assigned for such purposes worldwide.

Cataloguing-In-Publication Data
A catalogue record for this book can be obtained on request from the British Library.

Cover design
© 2010 Waterside Press. Cover features Cesare Beccaria by Giuseppe Bossi (original owned by National Library of Australia PIC U6362 NK2864 LOC 7291-7300). Design by www.gibgob.com.

UK distributor
Gardners Books, 1 Whittle Drive, Eastbourne, East Sussex, BN23 6QH.
Tel: +44 (0)1323 521777;
sales@gardners.com; www.gardners.com

North American distributor
International Specialised Book Services (ISBS), 920 NE 58th Ave, Suite 300, Portland, Oregon, 97213, USA.
Tel: 1 800 944 6190 Fax: 1 503 280 8832;
orders@isbs.com; www.isbs.com

Printed by
MPG-Biddles Ltd, Kings Lynn.

e-book
Cesare Beccaria The Genius of "On Crimes and Punishments" is available as an ebook (e-book ISBN 9781906534 936) and also to subscribers of Myilibrary and Dawsonera.

Cesare Beccaria

The Genius of *On Crimes and Punishments*

John Hostettler

❋ WATERSIDE PRESS

Also by John Hostettler

'Every student entering law school should have a copy and read it':
Criminal Law and Justice Weekly

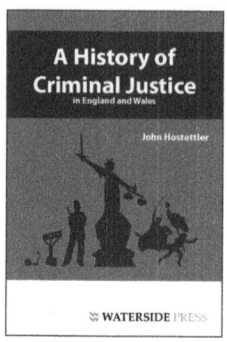

A History of Criminal Justice in England and Wales

An ideal introduction, charting all the main developments of criminal justice, from Anglo-Saxon dooms to the Common Law, struggles for political, legislative and judicial ascendency and the formation of the modern-day Criminal Justice System.
Paperback ISBN 9781904380511 | Ebook ISBN 9781906534790
Jan 2009 | 352 pp

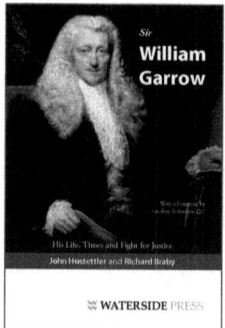

Sir William Garrow
His Life, Times and Fight for Justice
Co-author **Richard Braby**
Foreword **Geoffrey Robertson QC**

The 'Lost Story of William Garrow' formed the basis for the successful BBC1 TV prime-time drama series 'Garrow's Law'. This book tells the real story behind the drama: of Garrow's life, upbringing and fight with the legal establishment to change the face of the English criminal trial. 'A blockbuster of a book': *Phillip Taylor MBE, barrister.*
Hardback ISBN 9781904380559 | Ebook ISBN 9781906534820
Jan 2010 | 272 pp | 1st Ed.

Visit WatersidePress.co.uk

CONTENTS

Preface . . . . *ix*
    Watershed . . . . *ix*
    Visionary . . . . *xii*
    Cri de Coeur . . . . *xiv*
    Critique of Inquisition Procedure . . . . *xv*
    A Final Note . . . . *xvi*

About the author . . . . *xviii*

PART 1: BECCARIA'S LIFE AND TIMES *19*

  1: A Modest Man *21*
    Crime and Punishment *21*
    House Arrest *22*
    Academy of Fists *23*
    Thomas Jefferson *26*
    A Changing World *27*
    Retribution *29*
    Break with Friends *30*
    Death of Teresa *32*

PART 2: CONSIDERATION OF "ON CRIMES AND PUNISHMENTS" . . *35*

  2: Secret Accusations and Torture *37*
    The Effects of Secrecy *37*
    "Torture a Mercy" *38*
    Trial by Ordeal *41*
    Consecrated Cruelty *43*
    Bentham on Torture *46*
    Voltaire *48*

3: The Death Penalty ... 51
Ancient Origin ... 51
War Against Citizens ... 52
Deprivation of Liberty ... 54
Judicial Murder ... 56
Acceptance in Continental Europe ... 57
Impact in England ... 60
The Reverend Martin Madan ... 62
Archdeacon Paley ... 63
Criminal Law Commissioners ... 64

4: Criminal Law and Punishments ... 67
Reform of Criminal Justice ... 67
Penal Law ... 69
The Origins of Punishments and the Right to Punish ... 71
Interpretation of the Law ... 72
Consequences ... 73
Spirit of the Law ... 74
Obscurity of the Law ... 77
The Division of Punishments ... 78
Crimes of High Treason ... 79
Voltaire ... 80
Personal Security ... 80
The Purpose of Punishment ... 82
Prompt Punishment ... 82
Public Tranquility ... 83
Pleas of the Crown and Confessions ... 84

5: Crimes Difficult to Prove and Others ... 87
Presumptions ... 87
Adultery ... 88
Homosexuality ... 89
Infanticide ... 89
Suicide ... 90
Voltaire on Suicide ... 91

Smuggling *91*
Bankruptcy *93*
Leading Questions *94*
Oaths. *95*
Sanctuaries. *96*
Extradition *97*

6: Various Topics and Imprisonment *99*
Prosecutions and Prescriptions *99*
Criminal Attempts *102*
Accomplices. *102*
Evidence and Proofs of a Crime *103*
Witnesses *105*
William Garrow *107*
Imprisonment *108*
John Howard. *109*
Voltaire *109*

7: Other Punishments. *111*
Crimes of Violence *111*
Punishment of Nobles. *111*
Theft and Robbery. *112*
Ill-repute *114*
Rewards for Detaining or Killing Criminals *115*
Criminal Procedure. *116*
Voltaire *117*
Mildness of Punishments *118*
The Means of Preventing Crimes *120*
Science. *121*
Magistrates *123*
Certainty of Punishments–Pardons. *124*
False Ideas of Utility *125*
Family Spirit *125*
Voltaire's Commentary *126*

Part 3: Beccaria's Influence 129

8: Profound Impact 131
  The French Revolution and Adversary Trial 131
  Human Rights and Voltaire's Causes Celebres 134
  John Adams 136

9: Conclusion 139
  Success 139
  Revolution 141
  England 142
  Conclusion 144

Select Bibliography 146

Index 150

PREFACE

"As one reads history ... one is absolutely sickened, not by the crimes that the wicked have committed, but by the punishments that the good have inflicted."

Oscar Wilde[1]

Watershed

In the eighteenth century the death penalty excited widespread fear and horror in all European countries. Not without reason since the methods of state murder meant slow and painful strangulation on the gallows or the tearing apart of limbs in torture. It cast its ominous shadow everywhere. And not only for serious crimes. If proved, dozens of minor offences, such as stealing a handkerchief, would result in a sentence of death. No one was safe from it. To make matters worse, torture was practised in the many countries across the globe, whether considered civilized or not, that embraced the inquisitorial system of criminal procedure.

Secret accusations were endemic in France, Italy, Russia and many other countries. In these places punishments were determined, often behind closed doors, at the whim of magistrates and judges who often bought their way on to the Bench for which many of them were demonstrably unsuited. The judiciary was not independent but formed part of the executive, with the judges acting as prosecutors on behalf of the all-pervading state. The presumption of innocence and equality before the law were concepts unknown and an accused person was regarded as guilty unless he could prove his innocence. The burden of proof always lay on the defence. And a mere accusation was often accepted by judges as *prima facie* evidence of guilt. In essence, except in England which rejected torture and the inquisitorial system, the rule of law was disregarded in favour of judicial ferocity and cruelty. Indeed, the rule of law was not even recognised or understood.

---

1. *The Soul of Man under Socialism.* Works. (1963 edn) London, Spring Books. p. 922.

In this pitiless milieu the Italian Count Cesare Bonesana, Marquis of Beccaria set out to challenge the status quo. He wished to change the core of judicial thinking with its reliance on vengeance and long-standing customs from the past with a scientific approach based on reason and humanity. As a consequence, his seminal work *On Crimes and Punishments (Dei Delitti e delle Pene)* became the first theory of penal law and it continues today to provoke fresh thinking about criminal justice. Yet, so great was his success in the eighteenth century that we now accept the changes he inspired without much thought of the upheavals in penal thought, the legal system, and society generally, that were required to achieve them.

On Crimes and Punishments was a small book published in Livorno on 12 April 1764, at roughly the same time as adversary trial was beginning to emerge in England. Together, the book and adversarial trial raised issues of human rights to the forefront of penal thinking and created a watershed in the history of criminal justice in Europe when punishments were so brutal and harsh. Gradually, individuals were to acquire opportunities for defence that had been denied to them for centuries and almost immediately punishments were to be made more humane for those found guilty of criminal acts.

Generally speaking, many people at the time had despaired of any meaningful penal reform appearing and considered those advocating it to be wild visionaries. For example, Allan Ramsay, a Scottish painter and writer, wrote a letter to the Encyclopaedist, Denis Diderot, who had shown him a copy of Beccaria's book. In the letter he said that penal legislation could be considered only with reference to the particular needs of a country and that, "only a general revolution will ever make a legislature pay heed to the claims of philosophers" – meaning Beccaria. He continued,

> But since it would be an absurd folly to expect this general revolution, this general reconstruction, which could only be effected by very violent means, such as would be at least a very great misfortune for the present generation, and hold out an uncertain prospect of compensation for the next one, every speculative work, like *Dei delitti e delle pene,* enters into the category of Utopias, of Platonic Republics and other ideal governments; which display, indeed, the wit, the humanity and the

goodness of their authors, but which never have had nor ever will have any influence on human affairs...[2]

How wrong he was! Although reflecting a commonly held view, Ramsay completely misjudged the revolutionary impact Beccaria's book was to have as part of the Age of Enlightenment. Beccaria stands out in that period for his deep humanity and belief in human reason which inspired his attempt to perfect criminal law and procedure. The effects of his attacks on the terror underpinning the system of criminal justice were both immediate and influential in continental Europe. This included revolutionary France, until later when the introduction of the Napoleonic Code largely re-instated the medieval-type *Code Louis* of 1670.

Beccaria's native Lombardy, Portugal, Austria, Russia and France all abolished torture and reformed their criminal justice systems as a direct result of the potency of his onslaught. And in Tuscany the Grand Duke Leopold introduced sweeping reforms of the penal system along the lines advocated by Beccaria. Interestingly this led to a considerable reduction in the number of serious crimes. In all these countries Beccaria's pen brought about the destruction of a great deal of the prevailing system. His book was to take effect more slowly in England, where torture was not institutionalised and *habeas corpus* was a powerful deterrent to unbridled power. But it was assimilated in time and scenes of death on the scaffold of Tyburn Tree were gradually reduced.

Changes occurred at different speeds in different countries and, in addition to Beccaria's influence, the new English adversary model of criminal justice which gave prisoners rights of defence in court was adopted by the French revolutionaries in its entirety; juries, justices, adversariality, everything. The French revolutionary draftsman, Nicolas Bergasse, in a report published on 17 August 1789, said, "It is easy to see that no methods are talked about here except those furnished by the system of jurisprudence adopted in England and free America for the prosecution and punishment

---

2. Denis Diderot. (1875-1877) *Complete Works*. Paris. vol. iv. pp. 52-60. Cited in Coleman Phillipson. (1970) *Three Criminal Law Reformers: Beccaria, Bentham, Romilly*. New Jersey, Patterson Smith, pp. 36-37.

of offences … we cannot do better than adopt it without delay, ameliorating it, however, in certain details".³ This was anathema to Napoleon, however, and subsequently, in 1808, he secured the enactment of the *Code d'Instruction Criminelle* which revived the secret, inquisitorial pre-trial of the 1670 *Code Louis,* without the physical torture, while preserving only some aspects of the English style trial itself.

In particular Napoleon was entirely hostile to the jury system. Whilst dining with Charles James Fox in Paris in 1802, he told his guest that he could not bring himself to approve of trial by jury since, "it was so Gothic, cumbrous and might be so *inconvenient* to a government." Fox boldly responded that, "the *inconvenience* was the very thing for which he liked it."⁴ Napoleon's deeply authoritarian code became, and remains, an influential model of criminal justice around the world outside common law countries, "spreading its poisonous tentacles across Latin America, Africa, the Middle East, and the Far East."⁵

Visionary

Beccaria was born in 1738, the eldest son of an aristocratic family in Lombardy, then under the somewhat benevolent Austrian rule of Maria Theresa and her chief minister Kaunitz. Although Roman law predominated across continental Europe it was a German tribe, the Lombards, which gave its name to Beccaria's province (there was no unified Italy) and its similarly authoritarian laws survived, particularly in Milan. Moreover, at the time the Church was closely linked to the state and many sins were treated as crimes. But reform was in the air and soon in Lombardy the Church lost many of its privileges and the Holy Office of the Inquisition was abandoned. Under

---

3. A. Esmein. (1913) *A History of Continental Criminal Procedure with Special Reference to France.* London, John Murray, p. 408.
4. The Rev. George Croly. (1841) *The Life and Times of His Late Majesty George the Fourth.* London, H. Colburn. Cited in John Hostettler (1996). *Thomas Erskine and Trial by Jury.* Hook, Waterside Press (2010)..
5. Richard Vogler. (2006) *Criminal Justice and Due Process: A Global Revolution?* Unpublished Lecture in Lewes, Sussex.

the governorship of Count Firmian agriculture was encouraged, museums and libraries were expanded and works of public utility were carried out.

Nevertheless, the new liberal despotism drew back from touching the cruel penal laws and the constant use of torture, which remained as they were. Following secret allegations torture was still the accepted means of providing proof of guilt. It is true that torture could only be applied in regard to capital crimes but almost all crimes fell within that category. Other abuses and cruelties were also commonplace. Prosecutors and judges ruled the courts with unlimited discretion and corruption was endemic. "But how few", exclaims Beccaria in his book, "have examined and combated the cruelty of punishments, and the irregularities of criminal procedures, a part of legislation so elementary and yet so neglected in almost the whole of Europe". And how few have sought:

> by a return to first principles, to dissipate the mistakes accumulated by many centuries, or to mitigate, with at least that force which belongs only to ascertained truths, the excessive caprice of ill-directed power, which has presented up to this time but one long example of lawful and cold-blooded atrocity! And yet the groans of the weak, sacrificed to the cruelty of the ignorant or to the indolence of the rich; the barbarous tortures, multiplied with a severity as useless as it is prodigal, for crimes either not proved or quite chimerical; the disgusting horrors of a prison, enhanced by that which is the cruellest executioner of the miserable – namely, uncertainty;– these ought to startle those rulers whose function it is to guide the opinion of men's minds.[6]

Due process of law had no meaning and it was the worst features of the existing system that Beccaria was to destroy – and not only in Lombardy but throughout continental Europe.

Yet, as a person he was shy and retiring to a painful degree. He was an introvert with a dislike of life on earth which he likened to a desert. But that made the influence of his book even more amazing. His impact on Enlightenment Europe was both electric and awe-inspiring. The book has been heralded as, "a product of the period of enlightenment, it is a perfect

---

6. J.A. Farrer. (1880) *Crimes and Punishments including a new translation of Beccaria's Dei Delitti e Delle Pene.* London, Chatto & Windus, pp. 118-9.

expression of its ideals and aspirations in the penal sphere ... His critical remarks are followed by constructive proposals which, taken together, form a practically complete system of criminal law and procedure".[7] He was a visionary in the right place at the right time. His influence is still felt in the modern world and he is remembered as a champion of the cause of humanity in the criminal law.

Nonetheless, although we all benefit from his crusade to abolish cruelty from the penal law there remains a great deal of room for improvement and his work still repays careful study. Furthermore, with current powerful assaults on human rights, including again the use of torture and the death penalty in many parts of the globe, his arguments have a particular resonance that should be ringing in our ears at the present time.

Torture is now illegal in Europe but even today it still has its defenders who somehow manage to argue that although it is an evil it is an evil that is sometimes necessary. And it is still practised in other continents and during the presidency of George W. Bush the United States of America resorted to the hellish torment of waterboarding and other practices forbidden by the Geneva Convention. Equally, the death penalty, which is banned in Europe, is still wielded in some states of North America and in China as well as many other parts of the world.

Cri de Coeur

With friends Beccaria made a major contribution to the rebirth of his country as well as the cause of humanity and justice throughout the continent. Despite his shyness and sensitivity, his empathy with victims of injustice resulted in the small book that exploded in Europe with world-wide consequences. It was not the first protest against the bleak inhumanity of criminal law, nor was it merely a plea for some change. Rather, was it a *cri de coeur* for a complete reform of penal law giving rise to an intellectual movement for a more rational and enlightened society based on the social contract philosophy.

---

7. Sir Leon Radzinowicz. (1948) *A History of the Criminal Law and its Administration from 1750. The Movement for Reform.* London, Stevens & Sons Limited. vol. i. p.279.

It became the inspiration of a new and novel philosophical movement for the reduction of all punishments which quickly swept across continental Europe. In this it was in direct contrast with the theory of John Locke, so popular in England at the time, that the state should not restrict repressive laws which protected property rights.

Critique of Inquisition Procedure

Finding a secular, and not revelatory, origin of law, Beccaria rejected the Roman-canon procedure that reigned over continental Europe and argued that the natural and instinctive common sense of educated men was the only effective means of discovering the truth. He was lauded by Voltaire and his work resulted in widespread criminal law reforms being instituted not only in Italy and France but also by Catherine the Great of Russia, Frederick II of Prussia, the King of Sweden and Leopold of Austria. Nevertheless, he had his critics. The French jurist, Pierre-François Murat de Vouglans, described his views as a "contagion"[8] and endeavoured to defend the indefensible horrors of torture by claiming that, "the person likely to experience this torture must be regarded as more than half convicted of the crime, so that the danger of confusing the innocent with the guilty is not so much to be feared."[9] To which Voltaire witheringly responded that, "... half proofs are admitted, which is a palpable absurdity for we know that there are no half-truths. But at Toulouse they allow quarter and eighths of proof."[10]

What Beccaria was really offering was a detailed and systematic critique of inquisition process[11] that touched a cord among the peoples of Europe. He inspired a philosophical movement for the reduction of, and certainty in, all punishments that not only produced the abundance of new criminal codes across continental Europe but also served as an intellectual stimulus

---

8. A. Esmein. *A History of Continental Criminal Procedure with Special Reference to France.* Op. cit. p. 371.
9. *Ibid.* pp. 372-3.
10. Voltaire. (1766) *Commentaries on Beccaria's 'On Crimes and Punishments' by an Avocat of Provence.* Art. xxi.
11. Richard Vogler. (2005) *A World View of Criminal Justice.* Aldershot, Ashgate Publishing Limited. p. 47.

to the middle class in England that eventually would lead to the breakdown of the discretionary laws that were in place to protect the interests of a small but powerful aristocracy.

A Final Note

The idea of writing a book on Beccaria and *On Crimes and Punishments* was suggested to me by my wife, Joy. She has also read the manuscript and made a number of helpful suggestions and corrections for which I am extremely grateful. I remain, however, solely responsible for any errors that may remain.

In the main, I have used the translation of Beccaria's *Dei Delitti e delle Pene* by J. A. Farrer, published by Chatto & Windus in London in 1880. I am also indebted to the 4th edition of Beccaria's work, published in London by F. Newbery in 1775, and translated from the French with a Commentary attributed to Voltaire. This edition bears an unknown hand-written inscription which reads, "The first work that heralded a more humane spirit of criminal legislation." Francis Newbery's premises were well-known in London at the corner of St. Paul's Churchyard where he had taken over the publishing business on the death in 1767 of his father, John, who was a friend and publisher of Oliver Goldsmith and Samuel Johnson and the pioneer in publishing books for children. Unless otherwise indicated all extracts and quotations from Beccaria are taken from these two works.

I have not entirely kept to Beccaria's sequence of topics since I wish to lay stress upon issues such as torture and the death penalty which not only dominated the penal system in the eighteenth century but still deface many parts of the globe today. However, most of the topics are dealt with in short episodes following Beccaria's example. The book does not contain a literal reproduction of Beccaria's great work and at times I have paraphrased what he wrote to give his words and constructions a more modern meaning. It is hoped that, in essence, this book will be seen as an introduction to Beccaria's classic work and its enormous and fruitful influence.

Finally, in Beccaria's day there were no women judges, magistrates, voters or jurors and prisons were filled in the main, although by no means exclusively, with men. As a consequence, at the time it seemed natural, even to reformers, to use the word "men" and not "men and women". Fortunately, neither the reason nor the practice are any longer true but I considered it would be both clumsy and unhistoric to amend Beccaria's words in this way. I trust no women (or men) readers will be offended but if they are, I apologise.

John Hostettler
Rustington on Sea

October 2010

ABOUT THE AUTHOR

John Hostettler was a practising solicitor in London for 35 years as well as undertaking political and civil liberties cases in Nigeria, Germany and Aden. He sat as a magistrate for a number of years and has also been a chairman of tribunals. He played a leading role in the abolition of flogging in British colonial prisons and served on a Home Office Committee to revise the rules governing electoral law in Britain. He holds several university degrees and three doctorates.

His biographical works include those on the radical social reformer Thomas Wakley and legal icons Sir James Fitzjames Stephen, Sir Edward Carson, Sir Edward Coke, Lord Halsbury and Sir Matthew Hale.

He has since written a succession of acclaimed works for Waterside Press. These include *The Criminal Jury Old and New: Jury Power from Early Times to the Present Day*; *Fighting for Justice: The History and Origins of Adversary Trial*; *Hanging in the Balance: A History of the Abolition of Capital Punishment in Britain* (with Brian P. Block and a Foreword by former Prime Minister Lord Callaghan); the all-embracing *A History of Criminal Justice in England and Wales* and most recently, by way of the reissue of a work previously published by Barry Rose, *Sir Thomas Erskine*.

In 2009, his book *Sir William Garrow: His Life, Times and Fight for Justice*, co-written with Richard Braby (a descendant of William Garrow), rescued from obscurity the story of one of English law's forgotten legal giants, a story mirrored by the prime time BBC TV series 'Garrow's Law'.

PART 1:
BECCARIA'S LIFE AND TIMES

CESARE BECCARIA

CHAPTER 1

A MODEST MAN

Crime and Punishment

Born an Italian nobleman, the eldest son of an aristocratic Milanese family, Count Cesare Beccaria was an improbable law reformer. Nothing in his youth gives any suggestion of brilliance, yet, as we have seen, in 1764, while still a young man, he exposed the then existing bleak inhumanity of the penal law to startling effect in his book, *On Crimes and Punishments*. At the time he was only 26 years old and had no legal experience or knowledge other than a law degree. Equally, he had no empirical or academic knowledge of penal law or criminal procedure. This made the essay a work of advocacy rather than a deep theoretical study–but that was its strength. At the same time, he was able to invest his views on penal law with a social and philosophical spirit and content.

The book was published anonymously at first for fear of serious religious and government reprisals. A strong warning of religious persecution had, indeed, been given 16 years earlier when an unfortunate author named Giannone had been imprisoned in the citadel of Turin for 20 years because of some observations on the Vatican in his *History of Naples*.[1]

Indeed, the Inquisition forbade the use of Beccaria's book under pain of death and it was placed on the Index in 1766. One Church apologist, Padre Facchinei, a Dominican monk, in deriding the book as seditious, portrayed Beccaria as a "man of narrow mind, a madman, a stupid imposter, full of poisonous bitterness and calumnious mordacity". His own "broadmindedness" was revealed when he argued that secret accusations were the best, cheapest and most effective method of achieving justice. The book was stigmatised as having "sprung from the deepest abyss of darkness" and being

---

1. J.A. Farrer. (1880) *Crimes and Punishments including a new translation of Beccaria's Dei Delitti e Delle Pene*. London, Chatto & Windus, p. 15.

"horrible, monstrous full of poison, containing miserable arguments, and insolent blasphemies".[2]

Professional lawyers were not slow to join the Catholic Church in its onslaught on the book. In 1770 a lawyer from Provence in a work on criminal justice wrote that the book "tends to establish a system of the most dangerous and novel ideas, which, if adopted, would go so far as to overturn laws received hitherto by the greater part of all civilised nations".[3] And an advocate to the Parliament of Paris attacked Beccaria saying, "What can be thought of an author who presumes to establish his system on the *débris* of all hitherto accepted notions, who to accredit it condemns all civilised nations, and who spares neither systems of law, nor magistrates, nor lawyers"?[4]

But in Milan Beccaria was protected by Count Firmian, the liberal minister of Empress Maria Theresa, who wrote that the book was written with a great love of humanity and much imagination. And, notwithstanding Facchinei's vitriol, the book proved to be a brilliant indictment from which the crusade against capital punishment and torture was to take flight. Despite the attacks the acclaim was both immediate and enormous. The book went through six editions in 18 months and was translated into 22 languages. And Beccaria was described by the *Societé Economique* in Bern as "a citizen who had dared to raise his voice on behalf of humanity against inveterate prejudice". In his honour it also awarded him a gold medal.[5]

House Arrest

Beccaria was born on 15 March 1738 in Milan and was educated for eight years in the Jesuit college at Parma where he rebelled against the authoritarian methods of his tutors and failed to shine as a student. However, he did manage to take his law degree at the University of Pavia in 1758. Three years

---

2. *Ibid.* p.16.
3. J. A Farrer. *Ibid*, p. 18.
4. *Ibid.* pp. 18-19.
5. C. Cantù. (1862) *Beccaria e il Diritto Penale.* Firenze, p. 173. Cited in Sir Leon Radzinowicz. (1948) *A History of English Criminal Law and its Administration from 1750.* vol. i. London, Stevens & Sons Limited, p. 277.

later he desired to marry 16-year-old Teresa di Blasco but found himself in conflict with the wishes of his parents. Teresa's father Domenico di Blasco, an army officer, belonged to a noble family but was considered an insufficiently wealthy parent by Beccaria's father, the Marchese Gian Beccaria Bonesana. Unable to persuade his son to give up his love for Teresa he appealed to the magistrates to put Cesare under restraint, "in order that he might the more leisurely reflect on his condition". The justices complied but, at Beccaria's request, he was placed under house arrest in the family home. In the meantime, Teresa's father appealed to the Empress, Maria Theresa, stressing his own nobility, the dowry he was prepared to procure for his daughter, and the suitor's warm affection for her.

After being confined for three months Beccaria was set at liberty in February 1761 and promptly married his loved one. His father refused for some time to receive his daughter-in-law but was eventually reconciled with the couple.[6]

In 1762 their first child was born and named Giulia after Julia the heroine of John Paul Rousseau's novel *La Nouvelle Héloïse*.[7] However, this conflict with his father led to Beccaria dealing in *On Crimes and Punishments* with parental tyranny and the law-based hereditary system among noble families.

Academy of Fists

Despite his law degree, Beccaria's aptitude at first was for mathematics. However, on reading Montesquieu he turned towards economics and, in 1762, he published a tract on the disorder of the currency in the Milanese states with suggestions for its correction. At the same time he became close friends with the brothers Pietro and Alessandro Verri, and other young men from the aristocracy of Milan, and between them they founded an intellectual literary and discussion society called *L'Accademia dei pugni* (The Academy of Fists). Its purpose was to make fun of the stiff Italian academies of the

---

6. Coleman Phillipson. (1970) *Three Criminal Law Reformers: Beccaria, Bentham, Romilly*. New Jersey, Patterson Smith, pp. 4-5.
7. Richard Bellamy. (ed) (1995) *Beccaria: On Crimes and Punishments and Other Writings*. Cambridge, Cambridge University Press, p. xi.

time and give a practical core to philosophy. The name arose from a tendency for their discussions to end in fighting. They also set about attacking the powers of Lombardy's nobles and the Church, which was exempt from taxation. Another, and more serious aim, was to help reform the criminal justice system.

Count Pietro Verri, an economist and philosopher, was the more ambitious of the brothers and, ten years older than Beccaria, he became his mentor and inspiration. Verri returned to Milan after fighting bravely in the Seven Years War following a quarrel with his father, Gabriel, who held a high position in Milan but was opposed to reform. Through Pietro, Beccaria was introduced to the works of British and French philosophers including Hobbes, Hume and Helvetius. In fact, it was Pietro who persuaded him to write the essay to be known to the world as *On Crimes and Punishments* and when it was completed he edited it and broke down long chapters into shorter ones. According to Pietro:

> Beccaria began to write down some of his ideas on loose pieces of paper; we urged him on with enthusiasm, stimulating him so much that he soon got together a great quantity of them. After dinner we would take a walk, discuss the errors of criminal jurisprudence, argue, raise questions, and in the evening he would write. But writing is so laborious for him, and costs him so much effort that after an hour he collapses and can't go on. When he had amassed the materials, I wrote them out, arranged them in order, and thus made a book out of them.[8]

Clearly, it remained the work of Beccaria as Pietro was the first to acknowledge. Pietro was himself engaged on writing a history of torture whilst Alessandro, who wrote historical and literary essays, had first-hand experience of the appalling conditions at Milan prison where he held the position of "Protector of Prisoners". This involved visiting inmates and, where possible, assisting them with either their defence or their applications for mercy. The distressing conditions he witnessed in the prisons had a profound effect on him and he helped steer Beccaria towards penal reform. In fact, both

---

8. Carlo Casarti. (1879-81) *Lettere e Scritti Inediti di Pietro e Alessandro Verri*. Milan, vol. i, pp. 189-90. Cited by Henry Paolucci. (1963) *Beccaria: On Crimes and Punishments*. New Jersey, Prentice-Hall Inc., p. xvi.

brothers provided background material for Beccarria's relentless attacks on injustice.

Two years later the Verri brothers and Beccaria, inspired by *The Spectator*, Addison and Steele's literary magazine in England,[9] provoked a cultural and constitutional reform movement around their journal *Il Caffe* ("The Coffeehouse") which survived for some two years from 1 June 1764 to the end of May 1766. During this time it introduced into Italy the enlightenment thought of French men of letters such as the indefatigable Voltaire, and Diderot who was sometimes compared with Benjamin Franklin. Beccaria wrote for *Il Caffe* a "Fragment on Style", an article on "Periodical Newspapers", an essay on the "Pleasures of the Imagination" and a number of other contributions. But in return it also influenced *On Crimes and Punishments* which sought to bring about reform by the enlightenment discourse based upon the rational scientific spirit devoid of dogma that was expounded by the Encyclopaedists.

It became the first thesis ever published to attack the death penalty *per se*, as well as other savage criminal procedures, and to argue for criminal law to be rooted in rational principles. It is interesting to note that the philosopher Immanuel Kant defended the death penalty against Beccaria's attacks on retributivist grounds and also argued that Beccaria "often let utilitarian considerations stand in the way of considerations of justice".[10] However, it was precisely on grounds of utility that Beccaria asserted that the prevention of crime was more important than its punishment which should be "proportioned to the crime and determined by the laws."[11] Its primary purpose was to benefit society, not to torment offenders. At the same time, and more widely, he envisioned that an enlightened and liberal criminal justice system would be the core of a new social structure for free individuals.

---

9. Beccaria, in a letter written in 1766 to his translator, Morellet, stated that the *Spectator* had in England, "contributed so much to increase mental culture and the progress of good sense".
10. David Young. (1986) *Beccaria: On Crimes and Punishments*. Indianapolis, Hackett Publishing Company, p. xv.
11. Cesare Beccaria. (1775) *An Essay on Crimes and Punishments*.(4th edition) London, F. Newbery, p. 179.

Thomas Jefferson

Within eighteen months of its publication the book was translated into French by André Morellet in 1766 and was presented with an anonymous commentary, written in fact by Voltaire. Morellet had made a number of unauthorised and unhelpful changes although grudgingly they were subsequently approved by Beccaria who believed the translator to be his intellectual superior. The book was also translated into English and other languages and read by at least two of the founding fathers and future Presidents of the United States, John Adams and Thomas Jefferson. It had a crucial impact on the Constitution of the United States of America, its Bill of Rights and eventually the English criminal justice system. When the American War of Independence began in the mid 1770s there were in Pennsylvania nearly 20 capital crimes but by 1794, largely as a consequence of Beccaria's influence, only murder in the first degree led to the gallows.

Indeed, Jefferson read the work in the original Italian and copied long passages into his commonplace book.[12] However, even after the creation of the United States, in Jefferson's native Virginia English criminal law still reigned with offenders variously hanged, whipped, pilloried, branded and dismembered. But Jefferson was opposed to capital punishment for all crimes except treason and wilful murder and he introduced into the legislature a Bill for "Proportioning Crimes and Punishments in Cases Heretofore Capital". In some respects the Bill was flawed and it was eventually defeated by a single vote in December 1786. It was, however, approved when submitted again in 1796.

It is noteworthy, however, that in the Bill Jefferson set out three cardinal principles which he derived from Beccaria. First, since punishment is an evil in itself, it is justified only so far as it produces greater happiness through the reformation of the criminal and the future prevention of crime. Secondly, punishments more severe than necessary to prevent crimes defeat their object by "engaging the benevolence of mankind to withhold prosecutions, to smother testimony, or to listen to it with bias ...". Thirdly, crimes

---

12. Merrill D. Peterson. (1970) *Thomas Jefferson & the new nation.* New York, Oxford University Press, p. 124.

are more effectively prevented by the certainty than by the severity of punishment: therefore, certain penalties should be clearly associated with certain crimes and justice should be swift and sure, protected from judicial caprice and special dispensations of any kind.[13]

A Changing World

At the time of Beccaria's triumph a new world was coming into being with marked changes in social conditions, political theories, class relationships and people's attitudes to life and their fellow citizens. In civil society naked violence was diminishing. Public disquiet was asserting itself about slavery, prison conditions and the rights and status of the individual. These developments flowed from various sources including the Glorious Revolution, the rapid growth of capitalism in England and the explosive consequences of the European Enlightenment. It was an epoch of revolution. At the same time, and in sharp contrast with these deep and subtle changes in society, criminal jurisprudence was continuing to be constricted by the barbarous penalties of medieval times. There was a complete lack of principles of reason or justice in the criminal law. Penalties did not depend so much on the law as on the discretion or whim and bias of magistrates and judges. The ubiquitous death penalty was the issue around which every other aspect of the penal system turned. In Europe torture was applied daily. The ghastly practice by which men were broken on the wheel was common, as were branding and mutilation. An Englishman travelling in France witnessed an execution on the wheel in the following words:

> On the scaffold was erected a large cross exactly in the form of that commonly represented for Saint Andrew's. The executioner and his assistants then placed the prisoner on it, in such a manner that his arms and legs were extended exactly agreeable to the form of the cross, and strongly tied down; under each arm, leg, etc., was cut a notch in the wood, as a mark where the executioner might strike, and break the bone with greater facility. He held in his hand a large iron bar and in the first place broke his arms, then in a moment after both his thighs; it was a melancholy,

---

13. *Ibid.* p. 126.

shocking sight, to see distortions of his face; it was a considerable time before he expired.[14]

Such scenes filled Beccaria with horror, and after referring to the "enlightenment of this century", he comes to the crux of his thinking when he writes that,

> How very few men have examined and set themselves against the cruelty of punishments, and the irregularity of criminal procedure, a part of legislation so fundamental and so neglected through most of Europe. How few have blotted out, by a return to commonly accepted principles, those errors which have accumulated through the centuries, or have attempted at least to curb, with the force of accepted truth, the unbridled advance of ill-directed power, which, until our day, has exhibited nothing but one long example of cold, legalized barbarity.[15]

What is needed, he adds, is to bear in mind that laws have only one end in view: "the greatest happiness shared among the greater number". Not, according to Richard Bellamy, "the greatest happiness of the greatest number"–the principle that Jeremy Bentham was to develop into the doctrine of Utilitarianism.[16]

In his essay entitled the *Fragment on Smells* (1764) Beccaria defines the public good as "the greatest sum of pleasures, divided equally amongst the greatest number of people."[17] Nevertheless, Bentham acknowledged his debt to Beccaria. "Oh my master", he cried, "first evangelist of Reason, you who have raised your Italy so far above England and I would add above France ... You who have made so many useful excursions into the path of utility, what is there left for us to do? – Never to turn aside from that path."[18] And in reference to his concept of the value of different pains and pleasures he said

---

14. See Jeffry Kaplow. (1972) *The Names of Kings: The Parisian Laboring Poor in the Eighteenth Century*. New York, Basic Books p. 135.
15. A.P. d'Entrèves. (1964) Introduction to Alessandro Manzoni's *The Column of Infamy*: Prefaced by Cesare Beccaria's *Of Crimes and Punishments*, London, Oxford University Press, p. x.
16. See Richard Bellamy (ed). *Beccaria: On Crimes and Punishments and Other Writings. Op.cit.*, pp.xviii-xix.
17. *Ibid.* xix.
18. A. P. d'Entrèves. Introduction to Alessandro Manzoni's *The Column of Infamy. Op. cit.* p. xi.

that it was from *On Crimes and Punishments* that he drew the first hint of the principle by which the precision and clearness of mathematical calculations were introduced for the first time into the field of morals.

For the incisive mind of young Beccaria what was needed was the tearing up of Europe's old Roman-based penal codes and replacing them with a new spirit which he now inspired with a view to maximizing the happiness of each individual person. However, he was clear that this could not be achieved without law and government and it would involve each individual sacrificing part of their liberty and obeying the law in order to preserve maximum freedom for all. It also rested on the principle that laws had to promote human happiness and prevent unnecessary harm.

Retribution

The prime objective of punishment in Beccaria's day was retribution or revenge. This involved punishment equal to the offence and was generally referred to in the maxim *lex talionis* (an eye for an eye, a tooth for a tooth). Beccaria regards this as not only arbitrary but pointless and unjust, asking "Can the groans of a tortured wretch recall the time past or reverse the crime he has committed?" There should be no other purpose for punishment than,

> To dissuade the criminal from doing fresh harm to his compatriots and to keep other people from doing the same. Therefore, punishments and the method of inflicting them should be chosen that, mindful of the proportion between crime and punishment, will make the most effective and lasting impression on men's minds and inflict the least torment on the body of the criminal.[19]

In this respect Beccaria was expressing the utilitarian belief that discouraging people from committing crime, with an emphasis on deterrence, makes for a stable and just society. On the other hand, he also drew upon the retributive argument which caused some tension in his approach. Other stresses arose from both his religious beliefs and his desire to reduce the influence, authority and wealth of the Church. Hence he, and the other members of

---
19. David Young. *Beccaria: On Crimes and Punishments. Op. cit.* p. 23.

the "Academy of Fists", wanted to abolish entails, which tied up land for the aristocracy and made it inalienable, and mortmain which gave land to the Church in perpetuity. Both, they believed, restricted economic advance and a spirit of individual enterprise.

Equality before the law is sacrosanct for Beccaria. The wealthy, he believes, could often evade the law whilst the poor suffered its lash. This should not be tolerated and equal sanctions should be applied impartially in spite of birth or rank. Not only was this desirable in principle but it would also reduce the incidence of crime when it was generally observed that all citizens are treated equally. But this could be brought about only by a centralised state stronger than elites depending upon hereditary privilege.

These views brought down the criticisms upon him that he sought to destroy religion which held society together and that he ignored the inequalities which would arise from his economic proposals. However, his liberal philosophy of criminal justice was never restricted and legalistic but was set within a social and political framework. In fact, he "rejected the military virtues characteristic of a traditional landed aristocracy and the religious virtues of ascetic self-denial. Instead, he sought to encourage the values of a competitive, commercial society: love of economic gain, prudent calculation of self-interest, tolerance for diversity of opinion, and the cultivation of `luxury', or higher standards of living".[20]

Break with Friends

Beccaria's book was warmly welcomed by the French Encyclopædists. Voltaire was delighted when he read it and invited its author to visit him at home although, as it happens, the two never met. Voltaire, whom we shall mention on a number of occasions, was the foremost exponent of the leading enlightenment ideas of the time. Born François Marie Arouet in 1694, he later came to be the most loved and the most hated man in Europe. He had a penetrating wit and style which he used to attack the horrors of injustice. All of those, according to Benjamin Disraeli who decried, "pedants, and priests,

---

20. David Young. *Ibid.* p. xiii.

and tyrants; the folios of dunces, the fires of inquisitors, the dungeons of kings, and all our ignorance, and all our weakness, and all our folly". How then might he have responded to Beccaria's onslaught on all these which reared their heads in the criminal law?

Beccaria was also invited to visit Paris and did so with Alessandro despite being reluctant to leave his home and his wife for the six months it was planned he would be away. At the commencement of his journey he is said to have cried like a baby at leaving Teresa to whom he had now been married for almost six years. And when in Paris, his shyness, and preference for obscurity over glory, prevented him from mixing freely with the French intellectuals to whom he was introduced. Pietro Verri chided him with having a childish side to his character which detracted from the esteem to which he was entitled. Verri also believed the trip to Paris would cure him but in this he proved to be wrong. In writing to Teresa, Beccaria spoke of the great impression Paris had on him and continued:

> I have seen Frisi, D'Alembert, Morellet, Diderot, Baron d'Holbach with whom I have already dined. You cannot imagine the welcome, the politeness, the eulogy, the demonstrations of friendship and esteem with which my companion and I were received. Diderot, Baron d'Holbach, and D'Alembert show themselves particularly delighted with us. D'Alembert is a superior man, and at the same time very simple. Diderot shows enthusiasm and good nature in his ways. In a word, nothing is wanting to me except your dear self. All wish to do me favours, and those who pay me such attentions are the greatest men of Europe. All design to listen to me; no one shows the least air of superiority.... Remember that I love you tenderly, that I prefer my dear wife, my children, my family, my friends in Milan, and you chiefly, to the whole of Paris."

He begs her to take this as a literal truth and not as a mere compliment.[21]

His melancholy and homesickness continued to distract him and, as a means of returning home before his visit was scheduled to come to an end, he constantly stresses in his letters that he is in ill-health, which was to some extent true. Morellet wrote of the episode that, "Toward the end of his sojourn he was so irritated mentally and emotionally that he would close

---

21. Coleman Phillipson. *Three Criminal Law Reformers: Beccaria, Bentham, Romilly. Op. cit.*, p. 17.

himself up in his room at the hotel where ... I often went to keep him company, trying, without success, to calm him."[22] In the event he did leave the city early and returned home after abandoning a proposed visit to England and leaving behind him a distasteful impression. As Piero Verri told him, "all sorts of things are bound to be said about your character which I can darkly foresee and which you can imagine as well as I, if you reflect on it."[23]

He preferred a contemplative rather than an active life and at home after his return from Paris, his friends, already full of jealousy at his success turned against him and began to deride him. As a result he ceased to be part of the "Academy of Fists". Worse was to come when Pietro and Alessandro now endeavoured to take the credit for his work, and relations between them continued to worsen. Alessandro wrote to his brother that all his thoughts were turned to mortifying Beccaria and they both called him a madman and an imbecile. They complained of his want of gratitude, rejoiced to think his reputation was on the wane and hoped that his "golden book" was closed for ever.[24] This breach and its consequences may, in part, explain why he never built upon his early promise.

Moreover, in 1767 when the Empress of Russia invited him to St. Petersburg to assist her in preparing a new criminal code he declined to travel. Instead, he accepted appointment as professor of political economy in the Palatine School of Milan. Occupying the post for two years, his lectures on political economy were well-received although they were not published until after his death. In 1771 he became a member of the Supreme Economic Council of Lombardy on which Verri was already serving. Indeed, the Council had been established following the publication of their ideas.

Death of Teresa

On 14 March 1774, Teresa died after a long illness, aged 29 and leaving two daughters. Despite his passionate love of her, four months later Beccaria was

---

22. Abbé Morellet. (1823) *Mémoires*. Paris, French Library of Advocates. vol. i. pp. 167-8.
23. Cesare Beccaria. (1958) *Opere*. (ed. Sergio Romagnoli) Florence, Sansoni, vol. ii. p. 869.
24. J A. Farrer. *Crimes and Punishments including a New Translation of Beccaria's Dei Delitti e Delle Pene. Op. cit.*, p. 25.

married to Anna Barbo, the daughter of Count Barnaba Barbo, by whom he had a son, Giulio. It was as if he could not bear to be alone. Shortly before he had been appointed not only a councillor of state but also a magistrate and he was soon to serve on various commissions of inquiry, so he was not exactly idle. And in 1790 he became a member of a commission for the reform of civil and criminal jurisprudence in Lombardy which brought to fruition many of his proposals. His main achievement in life, however, was *On Crimes and Punishments* both for its transformation of penal law and its emphasis on the moral and social principles on which criminal justice should be based.

Beccaria died suddenly of apoplexy on 28 November 1794 at the age of 57. He had seemingly enjoyed a life of solitude and was largely unmourned at the time. Milan is famed for its beautiful cathedral, Leonardo da Vinci's "Last Supper" and La Scala Opera House. It also now has two statues of Beccaria. One is the bronze statue in the Piazza Beccaria which ironically stands on the spot formerly the site of the hangman's house. It is a 1914 replica of the original damaged marble sculpture of 1871 by Giuseppe Grandi. It is a fine monument. But that is all. In a sense this arises from the fact that Beccaria was indifferent to honours and, indeed, society. When the King of Naples called upon him at his home on two occasions he made sure he was out. His extreme shyness, which continued until he died, caused untold difficulties but as a writer he exhibited great moral courage in the land which established the Inquisition, and this shone through his work which is itself his lasting epitaph. Nevertheless, more public appreciation would be both well-deserved and welcome.

Giuseppe Grandi, monument to Cesare Beccaria in Piazza Beccaria in Milan, Italy.
Picture by Giovanni Dall'Orto, 29 January 2007.

PART 2:

CONSIDERATION OF "ON CRIMES AND PUNISHMENTS"

Bronze statue of Cesare Beccaria, by Giuseppe Grandi, on the monument to Cesare Beccaria in Piazza Beccaria in Milan, Italy. The monument stands on the spot formerly occupied by the hangman's house. It was inaugurated on 19 March 1871. Picture by Giovanni Dall'Orto, 29 January 2007.

CHAPTER 2

SECRET ACCUSATIONS AND TORTURE

The Effects of Secrecy

In continental European law secret accusations and torture went together like a horse and carriage. They were bedrock components of the inquisitorial system. Beccaria sees them as abuses consecrated by custom and resulting from weak government. And, he believes, they make men dishonest and treacherous. A suspected informer is seen by honest people as an enemy and as informers are everywhere men become accustomed to masking their true feelings. Moreover, as a consequence of hiding their feelings from others they at last get to hiding them from themselves:

> In the end, he asks, who can possibly defend himself against false accusations which are supported by tyranny's impenetrable shield of secrecy? Men become confused and ever busy saving themselves from the horrors that oppress them and about an uncertain future with no lasting pleasures of quiet and security. How among such men can uncorrupted magistrates be found?

How miserable a government must be, he says, where it perceives every citizen to be an enemy and preserves the public peace by taking away his peace if mind. And how is it pretended that secret accusations may be justified? In the interests, they say, of public safety and the security and the maintenance of the established form of government. But, how strange it is that a government which has immense power should fear its own citizens. Or is the safeguarding of the accuser the excuse? If it is that an accuser needs protecting the law does not even defend him sufficiently either. Are there to be citizens more powerful than the law, he asks? Montesquieu had said that public accusations were more suitable to republics, where a citizen's first desire should be the public good, rather than a monarchy in which that desire is feeble owing to the nature of the government itself. But what is really required are public prosecutors who openly accuse those who break the law in both republics and monarchies.

"I respect every government" writes Beccaria, "and speak of none in particular. Circumstances are sometimes such that to remove an evil may seem utter ruin when it is inherent in a national system. But had I to dictate new laws in any forgotten corner of the universe, my hand would tremble and all posterity would rise before my eyes before I would authorise such a custom as that of secret accusations."[1]

"Torture a Mercy"

As early as the sixteenth century, the great French essayist and humanist Michel de Montaigne wrote in his *Essay on Conscience* that putting a man to the rack was rather a trial of patience than of truth; that pain was as likely to extort a false confession as a true one; and that a judge, by having a man racked that he might not die innocent, caused him to die both innocent and racked.[2] Yet, for ages up to the end of the eighteenth century, criminal justice on the continent of Europe was based heavily on judicial torture. Leading jurists such as Damhouder of Bruges (1554) and Hippolytus of Marsailles (1524) produced gruesome legal tracts which, together with explanations of the law, demonstrated exactly how to torture a suspect effectively. They laid down complex doctrines which indicated the level of torture to be applied in accordance with the gravity of the alleged offence and the weight of *indicia*.[3] Damhouder, for instance, gravely suggested that:

> The good judge is always compassionate, and must take into account the youth or age of his patient and the state of his health, to ensure that his office be that of the good judge and not the bloodthirsty tyrant. He must start carefully and moderately, then rigorously, and finally very rigorously indeed, according to the gravity of the

---

1. J.A. Farrer. (1880) *Crimes and Punishments including a new translation of Beccaria's "Dei Delitti E Delle Pene"*. London, Chatto & Windus, pp 142-44.
2. Montaigne. (1718) *Cautio Criminalis*. Cited by J. A. Farrer. *Crimes and Punishments including a new translation of Beccaria's "Dei Delitti E Delle Pene. Ibid*, p. 31.
3. Richard Vogler. (2005) *A World View of Criminal Justice*. Aldershot, Ashgate Publishing Limited, p. 29.

crime and the degree of proof against the accused and the nature of his replies. He must take no notice of the screams, cries, sighs, trembling or pain of the accused.[4]

And similar views were still being expressed in Europe in Beccaria's day.

The great penal codes, such as Charles V's *Carolina* of 1532 or Maria Theresa's *Nemesis Theresiana* of 1767, came illustrated with graphic depictions of the use of the tools of torture. There was no such thing as an open trial and often there was no trial at all. In some jurisdictions, such as France after 1670, the prisoner was brought before the judges merely for the pronouncement of sentence. The situation in England was bad enough, trials being a very brief "altercation" with the judges in complete control, but there were no secret trials or institutionalised torture.

The Roman Catholic Church argued that torture was a mercy to the criminal since it purged him in his death from the sin of falsehood. Beccaria categorizes this as "a ridiculous motive for torture which should not be tolerated". He asks if pain, which is a sensation, could have any connection with a moral sentiment, which is a matter of opinion. "Perhaps the rack may be considered as the refiner's furnace." It is not difficult, he writes, to trace this senseless and absurd law to religion by which mankind is so generally influenced. And, he continues by saying, "We are taught by our infallible church, that those stains of sin, contracted through human frailty, and which have not deserved the eternal anger of the Almighty, are to be purged away, in another life, by an incomprehensible fire." In any event, as ill-repute is regulated not by laws or reason but entirely by opinion, torture renders the victim infamous and, therefore, it cannot take his disgrace away or purge him of sin.

To Beccaria the torture of a defendant during his trial is another cruelty that was sanctified by custom in most nations. It was used with three purposes in mind. First, on the pretext of making the prisoner confess to the crime of which he is accused and clear up alleged contradictions in his statements. Secondly, to discover his alleged accomplices. And thirdly, to discover other crimes of which he is not accused but might possibly be considered guilty.

---

4. Damhouder. (1554) *Rerum Praxis Criminalum*. Antwerp, chap. xxxvii. Cited in Vogler *ibid.*

But, Beccaria argues, no man should be judged a criminal unless he is found guilty in law. Nor should society deprive him of its protection until it has been proved that he has committed a crime – an early expression by Beccaria of the presumption of innocence although "proof" had a different meaning in those days. By what right, therefore, can a judge be allowed to inflict a punishment on a citizen whose guilt or innocence has not been decided?

A man, he says, is either guilty or not guilty. If shown to be guilty, he should be punished according to the law and torture becomes useless as his confession is unnecessary. If he is not guilty, an innocent man is tortured to no purpose. He deplores the concept that a person should be both accuser and accused and to make pain the crucible of truth, as if the test of it "lay in the muscles and sinews of an unfortunate wretch".

What is the political object of punishment, he asks? To which he replies that it is to intimidate other men. But is this answered by secretly and privately torturing both the guilty and the innocent? It is important that no crime should remain unpunished but the hidden exposure of a criminal is useless. An evil that has been done and cannot be undone can only be punished by society in so far as it may affect others who have hopes of escaping from the arms of the law. Though if it be true that there are a greater number of men who, from either fear or virtue, respect the laws than of those who break them, the risk of torturing an innocent man should be estimated according to the probability that any man will have been more likely, other things being equal, to have obeyed rather than broken the laws.

The law which encourages the use of torture is a law which says to men: "Resist pain; and if nature has created in you an inextinguishable self-love, if she has given you an inalienable right of self-defence, I create in you a totally contrary affection, namely an heroic, self-hatred and I command you to accuse yourselves and to speak the truth between the laceration of your muscles and the dislocation of your bones."

Trial by Ordeal

Beccaria believes that torture is a remnant of the ancient and savage legislation in which trials by fire, by boiling water and by combat were called judgments of God. So-called trial by ordeal was not, in fact, a trial at all but a form of torture. There was no human judge or jury. The verdict was in the hands of the Almighty. The only difference Beccaria can see between torture and trial by ordeal is that the results of torture depend upon the will of the accused whilst trials by fire and by water depend upon something physical and external. But that difference is only apparent, not real. A man on the rack, in the convulsions of torture, has it as little in his power to declare the truth as, in former times, to prevent without fraud the effects of fire or boiling water. Every act of our will is invariably in proportion to the force of the impression on our senses which cause it, and the sensibility of every man is limited.

As a consequence, declares Beccaria, the pain increases to such a degree that it compels the sufferer to use the shortest method of freeing himself from torment and to accuse himself of crimes of which he is innocent. So the very means employed to distinguish the innocent from the guilty, destroys all difference between them. In any event, unknown to Beccaria of course, modern research shows that trial by ordeal, in England at least, was so arranged that prisoners generally went free whereas torture inflicts untold injury and misery on victims both physically and mentally in order to ensure their death either by the sentence of the judge or under the torture.[5]

The aforementioned truths, Beccaria sees, are understood in England and Sweden but in other nations, in every age, there are innumerable instances of innocent persons confessing to guilt under torture. And, of course, weaker men will confess more quickly than stronger men. Nevertheless, although in England torture was contrary to common law it was exercised under the prerogative of the Crown as interpreted by the Tudor and Stuart monarchs who used it at their discretion. Letters from these monarchs, including

---

5. For trial by ordeal see John Hostettler. (2005) *Trial by Ordeal, The Legal Executive* journal, Milton Keynes, pp. 24-5; and also (2004) *The Criminal Jury Old and New: Jury Power from Early Times to the Present Day*, Hook, Waterside Press, pp. 19-21.

Elizabeth I and the council, specifically instructed the Lieutenant of the Tower of London to use torture to extract "confessions" of treason, murder and robbery.[6] Invariably, intense pain and suffering were inflicted by the rack and other instruments of torture until the victim was left barely alive. And *peine forte et dure,* which meant pressing to death by iron and stone in inhuman conditions, was not abolished until 1772[7] although it was used infrequently in the century before that date. In his *Second Institute,* Sir Edward Coke described what this judgment of penance as it was called meant to a prisoner in the following words:

> The man or woman shall be remanded to the prison and laid there in some low and dark house where they shall lie naked on their backs on the bare earth. One arm shall be drawn to one part of the house with a cord and the other to another part. The same shall be done with their legs and there shall be laid upon their bodies iron and stone – as much as they shall bear and more ... The following day they shall have three morsels of barley bread without any drink. The second day they shall drink thrice of the water that is next to the prison (except running water), without any bread, and this shall be their diet until they be dead. So they shall die by weight, famine and cold.[8]

But for all that, it was rarely used and torture was not permitted at English common law and was never institutionalised in England as was recognised and praised by both Voltaire and Montesquieu as well as by Beccaria himself. However, in practically all of continental Europe, far from the inquisitorial system seeking the truth as was, and often still is, claimed, proof of guilt of crime was sought almost exclusively from secret accusations and torments both ingenious and gruesome. Roman forms of proof were adopted, "which exalted the probative power of sworn eye-witness testimony and of the confession of the accused, often coerced by torture".[9] In this way, "the law encouraged and, indeed, often required, the torture of the accused in

---

6. David Jardine. (1836) *A Reading on the Use of Torture in the Criminal Law of England prior to the Commonwealth.* Delivered at New Inn Hall, Michaelmas Term. Reprinted in the *Edinburgh Review.* vol. 67. (April-July 1838).
7. 12 Geo. III. c. 20.
8. Sir Edward Coke. (1797) *Second Institute.* London, E. & R. Brooke, p. 217.
9. G. Fisher. (1997) "The Jury's Rise as Lie Detector". New Haven, 107 *Yale Law Journal.* p. 587.

order to produce a confession, which was considered of particularly high evidentiary value."[10] It was a denial of the presumption of innocence unless a person was proved guilty.

Consecrated Cruelty

Beccaria ridicules torture as a means of purging a man from disgrace and describes its use during the course of a trial as a "cruelty consecrated by custom in most nations". As we have seen, it was used to make a prisoner confess his alleged crime, discover his accomplices, or discover other crimes of which he was not accused. Beccaria urges that a man should not be judged a criminal unless he was found guilty. He exposes torture to ridicule when he asks how the truth could reside "... in the muscles and fibres of a victim in torture". It is, he continues, a certain method for the acquittal of robust villains and for the condemnation of innocent but feeble men. These inconveniences of this pretended test of truth are worthy only of cannibals. It is a test, he says, not entirely accurately, since crucifixion is undoubtedly torture, which the Romans, barbarous as they too were in many respects, reserved for slaves alone, the victims of their fierce and too highly lauded virtue. Of two men, equally innocent or equally guilty, the robust and courageous will be acquitted, the weak and the timid will be condemned, by virtue of the following exact train of reasoning on the part of the judge:

> I as judge had to find you guilty of such and such a crime; you A B, have by your physical strength been able to resist pain, and therefore I acquit you; you C D, in your weakness have yielded to it; therefore I condemn you. I feel that a confession exhorted amid torments can have no force, but I will torture you afresh unless you corroborate what you have now confessed.[11]

---

10. B.J. Shapiro. (1983) *Probability and Certainty in Seventeenth-Century England. A Study of the Relationships between Natural Science, Religion, History, Law and Literature.* New Jersey, Princeton University Press, p. 174.
11. J.A. Farrer. (1880) *On Crimes and Punishments including a new translation of Beccaria's Dei Delitti e Delle Pene. Op. cit.* p. 151.

To make the situation even worse, by the law a confession made under torture was of no avail unless it was confirmed by an oath made after it. And, should the accused not confirm his confession he was tortured afresh.

According to Beccaria the result of torture is a matter of temperament, of calculation, which varies with each man according to his strength and sensibility; so that by this method a mathematician might better solve this problem than a judge. That is, "given the muscular force and the nervous sensibility of an innocent man, to find the degree of pain which will cause him to plead guilty to a given crime."

The object of examining an accused man is to ascertain the truth. But this truth is difficult to discover from a man's air, demeanour or countenance, even when he is quiet. How much more difficult will it be, therefore, to discover from a man upon whose face all the signs, whereby most men express the truth, are distorted by pain. Every violent action confuses and causes to disappear those trifling differences between objects, by which one may sometimes distinguish truth from falsehood.

A strange consequence that flows naturally from the use of torture is, that an innocent man is thereby placed in a worse condition than a guilty one. This is because if both are tortured the former has every alternative against him. For either he confesses the crime and is condemned, or he is declared innocent, having suffered an undeserved punishment. But the guilty man has one chance in his favour, since, if he resists the torture firmly, and is acquitted in consequence, he has exchanged a greater penalty for a smaller one. Therefore, whilst an innocent man can only lose by torture one who is guilty may gain by it.

Another excuse made for torture is its alleged usefulness when applied to criminals who contradict themselves under examination. It is as if the fear of the punishment, the uncertainty of the sentence, the legal pageantry, the majesty of the judge and the state of ignorance common to both the innocent and the guilty are not enough to plunge into self-contradiction both the innocent man who is afraid, and the guilty man who seeks to shield himself. It is as if contradictions which are common enough when men are easy are not likely to be multiplied when the mind is perturbed and wholly absorbed in the thought of seeking safety from imminent peril.

Torture, again, is employed to discover if a criminal is guilty of other crimes besides those with which he is charged. It is, says Beccaria, as if the following argument were employed: "Because you are guilty of one crime you may be guilty of a hundred others. This doubt weighs upon me: I wish to clarify the situation by my test of truth: the laws torture you because you are guilty, because you may be guilty, because I mean you to be guilty."

Another pretext for torture is to discover an accused man's accomplices in crime. But as it is not a fit method for the discovery of truth how will it serve to disclose accomplices which is part of the truth to be discovered? If a man is forced to accuse himself he will more readily accuse others. In any event, it cannot be just to torture men for the alleged crimes of others. Will not accomplices be discovered from the examination of witnesses and the accused, and from the evidence and whole circumstances of the crime? In fact, from all the means which should serve to convict the accused if he is guilty? Accomplices generally fly immediately after the capture of a companion. The uncertainty they face condemns them to exile and frees the country from the danger of fresh offences from them, so torture is again unnecessary.

Another ridiculous reason given for torture is that it eliminates from a person ill-repute. In other words, Beccaria declares, a man judged infamous by the law must have his testimony confirmed by the dislocation of his bones. Such abuse should not be tolerated in the eighteenth century. In support of this torment it is suggested that pain, which is a physical sensation, releases from disgrace, which is merely a moral condition. Is pain, then, a crucible, and disgrace a mixed, impure substance? But disgrace is a sentiment, subject neither to laws nor to reason, but to common opinion. Torture itself causes real disgrace to the victim of it. Hence, the result is that by this method disgrace will be taken away by the very fact of its infliction!

It is not difficult to go back to the origin of this ridiculous law, says Beccaria, because the absurdities themselves that a whole nation adopts have always some connection with other common ideas which the same nation respects. The custom seems to have been derived from religious and spiritual ideas which have so great an influence on the beliefs of men, on nations and on generations. An infallible dogma assures us that the stains contracted by human weakness must be purged by an incomprehensible fire. Now disgrace is a civil blemish, and as pain and fire take away spiritual and incorporeal stains, why should not the agonies of torture take away the civil stain of ill-repute? Beccaria says he believes that the confession of a criminal, which courts require as essential to a finding of guilt has a similar origin. In the mysterious tribunal of repentance the confession of sins is an essential part of the sacrament. And this is accepted in times of ignorance.

For some reason Beccaria considers that these truths were recognised in ancient Rome where torture was inflicted, he says, only on slaves who in law had no personality. More to the point he states that they have been accepted by England, "a nation, the glory of whose literature, the superiority of whose commerce and wealth, and consequently of whose power, and the example of whose virtue and courage leave us no doubt as to the goodness of her laws." That was true of the rejection of torture to extract confessions but shows not only an example of hyperbole but also little understanding of England's "Bloody Code". Torture, he adds, has also been abolished in Sweden and is not deemed necessary in armies despite their being composed of the dregs of different countries.

Bentham on Torture

As will be seen, Beccaria thought capital punishment might be considered where an individual in custody had the power to endanger the security of the nation and cause widespread death.[12] This line of reasoning was followed by Bentham when he discussed torture. Wanting law to be an efficient instrument of social control led him into inconsistency on the question of torture. At first he assumed it was morally indefensible, but later he came to think that this was sentimental prejudice and that in some circumstances torture was easier to justify than other punishments.

For instance, the attainment of its purpose was plainly seen and it could instantly be made to cease. Although he did not remark that the sufferer usually could not be restored to his former condition. In fact, he actually accepted the justice of his earlier observations opposing torture unequivo-

---

12. Post, p.53.

cally but, departing from Beccaria, he came to believe that there were two occasions when its use might be justified.

It is helpful here to understand that Bentham worked from a narrow conception of torture which he defined as making a person suffer violent pain to the body to compel him to do, or desist, from something. Clearly this did not include mental torture and this constricted his thinking. Bentham said he wished to consider whether torture might usefully be used in place of other punishments which he thought caused greater physical hardship, although it seems likely that any that did that would themselves constitute torture. What, he argued, distinguished torture from other punishments was, as mentioned above, that the success of its purpose was plainly seen and it could instantly be brought to an end. Hence, he concluded that there were two cases in which torture might properly be used.

First, where the thing a man was required by authority to do was something in his power to do and which the public had an interest in his doing. In this case so long as he continued to suffer for not doing it he was sure not to be innocent. Curious examples given by Bentham of crimes where this might be applicable were incendiarism, aggravated murder and assassination for hire. In each of these cases it might, instead, be considered that a criminal trial was appropriate.

Secondly, where it was only probably in his power to do something and where, for not doing it, he might suffer although innocent, but where the public interest was so great that an innocent person's suffering was the lesser evil. This could arise only where the safety of the whole state was endangered. Professor Twining gives the following modern example as explaining Bentham's position: "It is believed that an atomic bomb has been placed somewhere in a major city with a timing device attached to it. X, who is believed to have information about the location of this bomb, has been captured",[13] but refuses to disclose the location of the bomb. According to Bentham he could be tortured in order to extract the information.

The difficulty is that Bentham was prepared to institutionalize torture in these cases without paying sufficient regard to the difficulty of preventing

---

13. See Professor Twining. (1973) "Bentham on Torture". *Northern Ireland Legal Quarterly*. No. 3. vol. 24.

its abuse. Not all Utilitarians could follow his acceptance of torture, limited though it was, and many preferred Beccaria's appeal to principles of justice and humanity in all cases.

Despite the strictures of the Church, Beccaria was to savour success when, as we have seen, torture was abolished in Lombardy, Austria, Portugal, Sweden, Russia and France as a direct result of his small book. In all these countries his work destroyed the prevailing system.

Nevertheless, Beccaria sees lesser punishments than torture and the death penalty as essential both to prevent society from plunging into chaos and to defend public liberty. But, equally, any punishment which is not absolutely necessary is tyrannical. The aim of punishment, he constantly averred, is solely to prevent the criminal doing further injury to society and to prevent others from committing similar offences. Such punishment should make a lasting impression on the minds of others with the least torment to the body of the criminal.

Voltaire

Voltaire, in his Commentary on Beccaria's book, claimed that all mankind, fearful of violence against the person, desired that those guilty of it should be punished. However, human compassion detested the cruelty of torture to extract a confession. A person not condemned would suffer a punishment more horrible than that which faced them if their guilt was confirmed. In England and some other countries, he said, torture had been successfully abolished. Why do others persist in their inhumanity merely because it is an ancient custom? "I am ashamed", he admitted, "of having said anything on this subject, after what hath been already said by the author of the *Essay on Crimes and Punishments*. I ought to have been satisfied with wishing, that mankind may read with attention the work of that friend to humanity." He questioned why the French who were proud of their politeness should not also pride themselves on their humanity.

Why retain torture as an ancient custom, he asked, when experience in England and other countries where it was not in use showed crimes were not more plentiful. It was absurd to inflict upon a man a punishment more horrible than he would face if proved guilty. And why should a man who forfeited his life also forfeit his estate and thus force his wife and children to beg for their bread because the head of the family had harboured a Protestant preacher or listened to his sermon?

Although torture was abolished in much of Europe in Beccaria's day, as indicated earlier it is still used in many parts of the world. Countries practising torture, such as China, and in the recent past the United States of America, directly undermine global humanity and all modern theories of human rights. Organizations such as Amnesty International should be supported in exposing them to the contempt and horror they deserve.

CHAPTER 3

THE DEATH PENALTY

Ancient Origin

Like torture, capital punishment has a long pedigree. To the best of our knowledge it was first promulgated for 25 crimes in the laws of King Hammaurabi of Babylon in the eighteenth century BC. Later, it appeared as the only penalty for crime in the Draconian Code of Athens and the Twelve Tablets in Rome. Crucifixion, burning alive and impalement were the common methods of execution. By Beccaria's time the death penalty was deep-rooted in continental Europe's history with appalling methods of execution such as the horrendous breaking on the wheel which was, as a means of death, connected with the secret trials and torture outlined in the previous chapter.

In England the "Bloody Code" meant death by hanging for over 200 crimes, many of them trivial such as theft of cash or an article such as clothing or food to a value of a shilling or more. Cutting down a tree or hunting in any forest or park with a blackened face also led to the gallows. For high treason the penalty was merciless. A man found guilty was drawn behind a cart to the place of execution, hanged and cut down whilst still alive, disembowelled and castrated, with his intestines burnt before his eyes and finally decapitated with the remainder of his body cut into quarters.

It was thought that for women this punishment was too severe and, if found guilty, they were burned at the stake after being tarred, although in many cases the executioner managed to strangle them before they were engulfed by the flames of the fire. Although not generally recognised by historians as torture because they were not used to extract confessions these punishments for treason were indeed a fearsome form of torment.

Claimed to have been a remnant of Norman policy the burning of women alive was said by Blackstone in his inimitable style to be out of "the decency due to the sex (which) forbade exposing and publicly mangling their bodies...".[1] This was written by Blackstone in 1769. In the same year Voltaire wrote of the original German introduction of the torments of the wheel in his *Commentary* to Beccaria's book. On England he wrote:

> Ingenious punishments to render death horrible seem rather the inventions of tyranny than of justice. In England they ripped open the belly of a man guilty of high treason; tore out his heart, dashed it in his face, and then threw it into the fire. And wherein did this high treason frequently exist? In having been, during a civil war, faithful to an unfortunate king; or in having spoken freely on the doubtful right of the conqueror. At length, their manners were softened; they continued to tear out the heart, but not until after the death of the offender...[2]

Here we have one writer, an apologist for English penal savagery, the other more enlightened. It may be just as well for Blackstone that Voltaire did not turn his pen to the tarring and burning of women, although it must be said that in general Voltaire compared the situation in England more favourably than penal law and torture of the continent.

War Against Citizens

Although others had opposed the death penalty, Beccaria was the first to mount an original and sustained critique of its use. The useless profusion of punishments, he says, by which men have never been made any better, has driven him to examine whether the punishment of death was really useful and just in a well organized society. He concludes unequivocally that a man should not be killed by the authority of the law. What kind of right can that be, he asks, which men claim for the slaughter of their fellow-beings? What man ever wished to leave to others the option of killing him? The death penalty, therefore, is not a right.

---

1. Sir William Blackstone. (1809) *The Commentaries on the Laws of England*. London, T. Cadell. vol. vi. p. 78.
2. Voltaire. (1775 edn.) *Commentary* to Beccaria's *Crimes and Punishments*. London, F. Newbery, pp.v-vi.

He further considers that capital punishment does not deter from crime and, as the only reasonable basis for punishment is its effectiveness as a deterrent the death penalty is not only immoral, it is useless. It is itself a barbarous act of violence and an injustice since it renders an act legitimate in payment for an equivalent act of violence. Moreover, it is harmful to society in reducing sensitivity to human suffering. Countries and times most notorious for the severity of punishments, he declares, are always those in which the most bloody and inhuman actions and the most atrocious crimes are committed; for the hand of the legislator and that of the assassin are directed by the same spirit of ferocity.[3] The death penalty is the war of a whole nation against a citizen whose destruction it considers necessary or expedient and useful for the general good. But, execution is transient whereas long periods of imprisonment are more effective as a deterrent.

As indicated in the *Preface* to this work, Beccaria sees society as held together by the social contract which was made between rulers and ruled in order to rise above the barbarism which existed in pre-history when there were no laws. Punishment of crimes is necessary to restrain men from invading the freedom of others that is established by laws. But every punishment not based on absolute necessity is tyrannical.

Not that such a contract has actually ever been entered into and unfortunately this theory led Beccaria into some convoluted language as will be seen. He was not always concise and sometimes his writing can be obscure. He is clear, however, that no one ever gave to others the right of taking away his life. By what right have men to authorise others to cut the throats of their fellow creatures, he asks? "Why he has not the right even to kill himself".[4] And not having this right himself, how could he transfer it to another person or to society?

In only two cases does he accept that capital punishment might be necessary. The first is when, though deprived of his liberty, a man still has such power and connections that he can endanger national security. That is when his existence might produce a dangerous revolution in the established form

---

3. C. Beccaria. (1775) *An Essay on Crimes and Punishments with a Commentary Attributed to Monsieur De Voltaire. Translated from the French.* 4th edn. London, F. Newbery, p. 99.
4. At the time suicide was a crime and even now there is no *right* to kill oneself.

of government. But, even then, only when disorder or anarchy has displaced the rule of law. Otherwise the punishment of death is pernicious to society because of the example of barbarity it presents. The second case might arise if death were the real and only restraint for diverting others from committing crimes. It appears absurd to him that the laws which express the public will which detest and punish homicide should, in order to prevent murder, commit murder themselves? And, in order to dissuade citizens from assassination, actually command public assassination. No advantage in moral policy could be lasting, he asserts, unless it is founded on the indelible sentiment of the heart of man.

Deprivation of Liberty

Beccaria considers that the duration of punishment has more impact on men's minds than the intensity of its pain. Our sensibility is more easily and permanently affected by very slight but repeated impressions than by a strong but brief shock. When the death penalty is carried out in public before vast crowds, capital punishment, he writes, becomes a spectacle for the majority of mankind, and a subject for compassion and abhorrence for others. The minds of the spectators are more filled with these feelings than with the wholesome terror the law pretends to inspire. But in moderate and continuing penalties the latter is the predominant feeling, because it is the only one. The limit which the legislator should affix to the severity of penalties, appears to lie in the first signs of a feeling of compassion becoming uppermost in the minds of the spectators, when they look upon the punishment rather as their own than as that of the criminal.

The most powerful effect is not the terrible but brief spectacle of a criminal's death but the prolonged example of a man deprived of his liberty. Death is viewed with a slight impression and in a distant manner. But the example provided by deprivation of liberty constantly works on the mind as a general deterrent. Nonetheless, the penalty should last for only so long as is needed to deter the criminal himself and others. In order that a punishment might be just, it has to contain only such degrees of intensity as are sufficient to deter men from crimes.

No one, he thinks, would choose total loss of freedom whatever gain the crime might bring. Hence, life imprisonment would deter more than a death sentence. Very many men face death calmly and firmly, some from fanaticism, some from vanity which almost always goes with a man to the tomb. Others face death calmly in a last desperate attempt to die or to escape from their misery. But neither fanaticism nor vanity can survive among fetters and chains or in a cage of iron. The unfortunate person thus punished is so far from ending his miseries that with his punishment he only begins them. The spirit can cope with violence and passing pain better than unending weariness. Imprisonment with hard labour terrifies the public more than judicial execution since the latter lasts for a terrible moment whilst the former lasts for a considerable time.

With capital punishment each example remains a single one; with imprisonment a single crime presents numerous and lasting warnings to others. To objections that life imprisonment is as painful as death, and therefore equally cruel, Beccaria replies that taking into consideration all the unhappy moments of imprisonment it will perhaps be more painful than death but whilst these moments are spread over a whole lifetime death exercises all its force in a single moment. There is also this advantage in imprisonment, that it has more terrors for him who sees it than for him who suffers it. This is because the former thinks of the whole total of unhappy moments whilst the latter, by the unhappiness of the present moment, has his thoughts diverted from that which is to come. All evils are magnified in imagination, and every sufferer finds resources and consolations unknown to and not believed in by spectators who substitute their own sensibility for the hardened soul of a criminal.

Beccaria examines the reasoning of a robber or assassin who is deterred from breaking the law only by thoughts of the gibbet or the wheel. His conduct, he concludes, is influenced by vaguely understood principles. Such a person asks:

> what are these laws, that I am supposed to respect, which make so great a difference between me and a rich man? He refuses me the farthing I ask of him, and excuses himself, by bidding me have recourse to labour with which he is not acquainted. But who made these laws? The rich and the great who never visit the miserable hut

of the poor, who have never seen him dividing a piece of mouldy bread, amidst the cries of his famished children and the tears of his wife.

Let us break those ties, he cries, which are fatal to the bulk of mankind and useful only to a few indolent tyrants. Let us attack injustice at its source. I will return to my natural state of independence. I shall live free and happy on the fruits of my courage and industry. A day of pain and repentance may come, but it will be short; and for an hour of grief I shall enjoy years of pleasure and liberty.

Beccaria now turns to religion:

Religion, he declares, then presents itself to the mind of the criminal facing death and promising him almost a certainty of happiness upon the easy terms of repentance, considerably diminishes for him the horror of the last scene of the tragedy. But he who foresees that he must pass a great number of years, or perhaps the remainder of his life, in servitude and suffering before the eyes of fellow citizens with whom he was living in freedom and friendship, the slave of those laws that once protected him, makes a useful comparison of all those circumstances with the uncertain result of his crimes, and the shortness of the time in which he shall enjoy their fruits. The ever present example of those whom he actually sees the victims of their own imprudence, impresses him much more strongly than the sight of a punishment which hardens rather than corrects him.[5]

Judicial Murder

To Beccaria the punishment of death is injurious to society for the example of barbarity it presents. If human passions in wars teach men to shed the blood of their fellow men the laws, which are intended to moderate human conduct, should not extend that savage example, particularly when carried out with formal pageantry. Is it not absurd, he asks again, that laws which punish homicide should, in order to prevent murder, themselves publicly impose murder? What must men think when they see magistrates and grave ministers, with calm indifference, causing a criminal to be dragged to death and, while the miserable wretch trembles in agony awaiting the fatal blow,

---

5. Cesare Beccaria. *An Essay on Crimes and Punishments with a Commentary Attributed to Monsieu De Voltaire. Translated from the French. Op. cit.*

the judge who condemned him by exerting his authority enjoys the comforts and pleasures of life. They will say murder, which they present as a horrible crime, is practised by criminals without repugnance or remorse. Let us then follow their example. Such is the fatal, though absurd, reasoning of men who are disposed to commit crimes among whom the abuse of religion is more potent than religion itself.

The examples given by history in all nations which have inflicted the punishment of death upon some crimes, are of no avail before truth, against which there is no fixed duration of time. Indeed, the history of mankind illustrates an immense sea of errors among which a few truths, in confusion and at long intervals, float on the surface. Human sacrifices were once common to all nations yet who for that reason will defend them?

That some few states, and for a short time only, says Beccaria, should have abstained from inflicting death rather favours his argument than otherwise. It is in keeping with the lot of all great truths whose duration is but of a lightening flash in comparison with the long and dark night that envelops mankind. The happy time has not yet arrived when truth, as error has previously done, shall belong to the majority of people.

Claiming that he is aware that his voice, as that of a philosopher, is too weak to be heard amid the clamours of the multitude he nevertheless believes that if the truths he is expounding should force their way to the thrones of princes they should know that they are backed by the secret wishes of all mankind. Such sovereigns who accept these truths, he adds, should know that their fame will outshine the glory of conquerors.

The truths he was expressing were indeed to be speedily adopted in many countries across Europe.

Acceptance in Continental Europe

For instance, in Russia, Catherine I abolished both the gallows and the wheel. Catherine II went further in desiring to establish a reformed and uniform penal code and asked Beccaria to go to Russia and introduce the reforms in person. Although he failed to do so, to secure reform, in 1767, she called to Moscow some 650 deputies from all parts of Russia. In the instructions read to the assembly, as a basis for the proposed codification, the principles set out clearly recall Beccaria's doctrines, not only in their spirit, but even in their letter. Some of her maxims of juridical and political philosophy, as well as common sense, were as follows:

- Laws should only be considered as a means of conducting mankind to the greatest happiness.
- It is incomparably better to prevent crimes than to punish them.
- The aim of punishment is not to torment sensitive beings.
- All punishment is unjust that is unnecessary to the maintenance of public safety.
- In methods of trial the use of torture is contrary to sound reason. Humanity cries out against the practice and insists on its abolition.
- Judgment must be nothing but the precise text of the law, and the office of the judge is only to pronounce whether the action is contrary or conformable to it.
- In the ordinary state of society the death of a citizen is neither useful nor necessary.[6]

The influence of Beccaria is apparent in every line although, no doubt, the maxims were not faithfully followed in every part of Russia's wide dominions. Nevertheless, the general influence these proposals had was so great that they were translated into Latin, German, French and Italian.

In Tuscany, where robberies and murders were endemic despite harsh penal laws, the Grand Duke Leopold resolved in 1786 to adopt Beccaria's proposals. He published a criminal code which proportioned punishments to crimes, abolished mutilation and torture, reduced the scope of treason, and abolished capital punishment even for murder. In consequence, only five murders were committed in 20 years whilst in Rome, where death continued to be inflicted with great pomp and ceremony, as many as 60 were committed within the space of three months.[7]

---

6. J.A. Farrer. (1880) *Crimes and Punishments including a new translation of Beccaria's Dei Delitti e Delle Pene*. London, Chatto and Windus, p. 33.
7. *Ibid.* pp. 35-36.

When the penal code of Joseph II was prepared in 1785, in order to substitute lesser punishments for hanging, it was issued in secret to ensure that the general public should be unaware of the change. No doubt the authorities believed that when it comes to the scaffold public opinion always seems to lag behind the legislators. Furthermore, the authorities were concerned that in so far as the provisions of the code became known it should not be thought they owed anything to Beccaria.

"In the abolition of capital punishment", said Kaunitz, "his Majesty pays no regard at all to the principles of modern philosophers, who, in affecting a horror of bloodshed, assert that primitive justice has no right to take from a man that life which Nature only can give him. Our sovereign has only consulted his own conviction, that the punishment he wishes substituted for the capital penalty is more likely to be felt by reason of its duration, and therefore better fitted to inspire malefactors with terror."[8] There was no public recognition that this was at the root of Beccaria's philosophy on capital punishment.

In France, the Revolution put an end to the death penalty for over one hundred different offences. And in Pennsylvania the penal code provided in 1794 that the only crime that should involve the punishment of death was murder.

Before Beccaria's onslaught, not only were secret accusations and torture the rule in continental countries using an inquisitorial system of trial, but evidence was often flimsy or non-existent and the judges had unlimited discretion as to what punishment to impose. In this context Beccaria's proposals were not only humane but revolutionary as the Catholic Church immediately recognised. As we have seen, their impact spread like wildfire throughout the continent where more liberal penal codes were speedily enacted although marred in many cases by the continuance of appalling alternative punishments.

It is interesting to remember that in 1790 Beccaria sat on a commission appointed to recommend reforms in the penal system of Lombardy.[9] On

---

8. *Ibid.* p. 36.
9. Coleman Phillipson. (1970) *Three Criminal Law Reformers: Beccaria, Bentham, Romilly.* Montclair, New Jersey, Patterson Smith Reprint Series, p. 72-3.

capital punishment a minority report was presented by Beccaria, Scotti and Risi. It suggested the almost total abolition of the death penalty and its replacement by penal servitude of a severity to be determined by the gravity of the offence. Following Beccaria they argued that the death penalty being unnecessary is not just, that it is not sufficiently deterrent and it is irreparable.

Impact in England

Beccaria's impact was not felt immediately in England, however, where the defence of property was still the principal purpose of punishment. In fact, the second half of the eighteenth century witnessed a strengthening of the penal laws and an extension in the incidence of the death penalty. Times were hard and a rapid impoverishment of the poor was perceived as a cause of a growth in crime. Describing the hunger, cold nakedness, filth and disease of whole families Henry Fielding unfeelingly concluded that, "they starve, and freeze and rot among themselves; but they beg, and steal and rob among their betters".[10]

In his great treatise on English law Blackstone merely mentioned Beccaria in passing (but Beccaria's book had been published only the year before) and believed that punishment should be increased where temptation was greater – presumably as a deterrent. Thus theft of a handkerchief from the person should result in death, whilst theft of a more valuable load of hay merited transportation.[11] Nevertheless, he did complain about the extent of capital punishment and, with Beccaria, argued that the certainty of punishment was a greater deterrent that its severity. Moreover, Sir William Holdsworth argues that Beccaria's book helped Blackstone to crystallize his ideas and that it was Beccaria's influence "which helped to give a more critical tone to his treatment of the English criminal law than to his treatment of any other part of English law".[12]

---

10. Henry Fielding. (1753) *A Proposal for Making an Effectual Provision for the Poor, for amending their morals, and for rendering them useful members of the society.* Dublin, John Smith and Richard James, p. 10.
11. Sir William Blackstone. (1809) *Commentaries on the Laws of England.* vol. iv, London, Cadell,
12. Sir William Holdsworth. (1938) *A History of English Law.* London, Methuen & Co. Ltd.,

Samuel Romilly acknowledged a debt to Beccaria in his first speech in the House of Commons on criminal law reform. And, literature also played its part. Horace Walpole deplored "the monthly shambles at Tyburn", where executions were carried out, as a "scene that shocked humanity".[13] In advocating the restriction of capital punishment to cases of murder Dr Johnson declaimed that "to equal robbery with murder is to reduce murder to robbery, to confound in common minds the gradations of iniquity, and incite the commission of a greater crime to prevent the detection of a less".[14] And Oliver Goldsmith, whilst accepting that murder should be a capital crime, questioned the right of the state to punish offences against property with death. At the same time he wrote of prisons as places which "enclose wretches for the commission of one crime and return them, if returned alive, fitted for the perpetration of thousands".[15]

In 1771 William Eden, later Lord Auckland, published *Principles of Penal Law* in which he sought to win support for the ideals of Beccaria by advocating that vindictive justice was utterly appalling. He held that severe penalties were the instruments of despotism and that punishments that were too severe led to impunity. The infliction of death, he said, was not a proper mode of punishment but a last resource, in the case of absolute necessity, in clearing from society those who threatened public safety. In words reminiscent of Beccaria, he said, "Penal laws are to check the arm of wickedness, but not to wage war with the natural sentiments of the heart".[16] Eden was supported by Samuel Romilly who had an even more significant impact in inspiring a generation of reformers, who ultimately achieved a revolutionary breakthrough in England in the mid-nineteenth century when the death penalty was preserved only for murder and treason.

Sweet & Maxwell. vol. xi. p. 578.
13. Horace Walpole. (1822) *Memoirs of the Last Ten Years of George II's Reign*. London, John Murray, vol. i. p. 224
14. Samuel Johnson. (1751) *The Rambler*. No. 114.
15. Oliver Goldsmith. (1752) *The Vicar of Wakefield*. London, The Folio Society 1971 edn.ch. 27 p. 173.
16. William Eden. (1771) *Principles of Penal Law*. London, B. White and T. Cadell, pp. 12, 14, 21, 22.

The Reverend Martin Madan

Efforts to oppose the death penalty in England received a serious setback in 1784 and 1785 with the publication of two books. The first was written by the Rev. Martin Madan and entitled, *Thoughts on Executive Justice*. Madan was himself a barrister, cousin of the poet William Cowper and, perhaps surprisingly in the light of his views, a Quaker. He believed that all capital laws should rigidly and invariably be enforced. The rigour of the criminal laws, he wrote, was extremely beneficial. Severity produced fear and made an example of the guilty. Hence the punishment of the law should be executed relentlessly in every case without any relaxation. The book had a considerable influence on the judges which produced a temporary bloodbath. In the year before it was published 51 people were executed in London alone and in the year following publication the number had risen to 97.

Sir Samuel Romilly, who accepted the principles of Beccaria and spent his life trying to mitigate the severity of the penal laws, stigmatized capital punishment as a lottery of justice and attacked Madan's demand that all capital laws should be rigidly enforced as being foolish and inhuman.

He was stung in reply to publish in 1786 an essay entitled *Observations on a Late Publication Intitled, Thoughts on Executive Justice*[17] in which he argued for imprisonment instead of death for most felonies. Ahead of most of his contemporaries he believed that excessive severity increased crime rather than deterred it. "Madan's relentlessness", he wrote, "breathes a spirit contrary to the genius of the present times." His doctrine, he said, was not supported by dispassionate argument; instead he used far-fetched hyperboles, ferocious language, and "all the most specious colouring of rhetoric". Only one hundred copies of Romilly's reply were sold but he sent a copy to each of the judges and the number of executions fell back.

It was Madan's book that prompted Romilly to make reform of the criminal law his main purpose in public life and through his untiring work in Parliament, he inspired a generation of penal reformers who ultimately achieved a revolutionary breakthrough in the nineteenth century. His mem-

---

17. Samuel Romilly. (1786) London.

ory is undimmed and he endures as a renowned figure in the history of penal law reform.

Archdeacon Paley

The second book was written by the influential Archdeacon Paley who unfurled the ideological colours of a criminal law system actually centred on capital punishment.[18] Justice, proclaimed this Doctor of Divinity in his *Moral and Political Philosophy*, must be left to God. To prevent crimes man's laws should provide capital punishment for every crime which, under any circumstances, might merit death. The judges should then act with discrimination in sentencing but by means of this threat hanging over the crimes of many, "the tenderness of the law cannot be taken advantage of." If an innocent person was hanged as a result he or she should be considered as falling for their country, since the general effect was to uphold the welfare of the community. "Acting the patriot for others", grimly observed Romilly. Not everyone saw the law of the time as tender but Paley described his design for a multiplicity of capital offences as being based on "wisdom and humanity". And, as an example of such humanity, he went on to advocate that murderers should meet death by being thrown into a den of wild beasts where they would perish in a manner dreadful to the imagination but concealed from view!

One may well wonder what kind of world Paley was living in, yet his advocacy was to have a profound influence in England for almost a century. His book was dedicated to the Bishop of Carlisle, the father of Lord Ellenborough, whose speeches in the House of Lords and in court both defended and followed Paley's doctrine. The noble lord successfully opposed every effort to humanise the criminal law of his day and in the House of Lords he argued that only terror could prevent crime and he helped ensure that the House of Commons' Bills ameliorating the criminal law were defeated on occasion after occasion. When Romilly endeavoured to refute Paley's

---

18. William Paley. (1785 edn) *Principles of Moral and Political Philosophy*. In *The works of W. Paley*. (1825) vol. vi. Edinburgh, Peter Brown and T. & W. Nelson, chap. 9, p. 526.

philosophy in the House of Commons, William Windham MP responded that it "had done more for the moral improvement of mankind than perhaps the writings of any other man that had ever existed."[19] According to T. R. Birks, Paley's book "reigned widely in England for nearly half a century as the best modern work on ethical science".[20] It was adopted as a textbook by Cambridge University and ran through 15 editions in Paley's own lifetime.

An example of the severity of penal law in England at the time is seen in a case in 1777 when a girl aged 14 years lay in Newgate Prison under sentence to be burnt alive for false coining, because some whitewashed farthings, that were to pass for sixpences, were found in her possession. A reprieve only came just as the cart was ready to take her to the stake. Not until 1790 was the law abolished by which women were liable to be burnt publicly at the stake for high or petit treason.[21]

Criminal Law Commissioners

However, in appealing to reason and the principle of utility, Beccaria had a considerable influence on Jeremy Bentham who adopted most of Beccaria's theses and developed them into his own brand of criminal law reform. Bentham declared that Beccaria was, "the father of *Censorial Jurisprudence*". This meant he was, "the first thinker to attempt a critical or 'censorial', as opposed to a merely expository, account of the law, which sought to demystify and correct the prejudices and confused reasoning that guided most contemporary legal decision making."[22] In addition to Eden and Romilly it was through Bentham and his followers that the ideas of Beccaria were absorbed into England's criminal justice system.

Finally, in the nineteenth century, Beccaria's ideas were praised by the Benthamite Criminal Law Commissioners, appointed on the instigation of

---

19. *Hansard.* [15] col. 371.
20. T.R. Birks. (1874) *Modern Utilitarianism: or The systems of Paley, Bentham and Mill examined and compared.* London, Macmillan & Co., p. 48.
21. J. A. Farrer. *Crimes and Punishments including a new translation of Beccaria's Dei Delitti e Delle Pene. Op. cit.* p. 53.
22. Richard Bellamy. (ed) (2003). *Beccaria: On Crimes and Punishments and Other Writings.* Cambridge, Cambridge University Press, pp. xvi-xvii.

Lord Brougham after the great Reform Act of 1832, who gave effect to them in the draft codes of criminal law they produced. The five commissioners, selected by Lord Brougham, were Andrew Amos, Henry Bellenden Ker, Thomas Starkie, William (afterwards Mr. Justice) Wightman and John Austin. All were advanced liberal reformers and they assisted Lord John Russell in preparing legislation to allow prisoners to be fully represented by counsel and to substantially reduce the incidence of the death penalty. In their Second Report they described Beccaria's theories as "sound and conclusive principles" of penal legislation and they used them as a framework for their own progressive views and proposals on the death penalty and other punishments.[23]

It was in the euphoria that succeeded the passing of the Reform Act that in 1832 stealing a horse or a sheep ceased to be a capital crime. Also ceasing to be capital crimes were breaking into a house (1833), returning prematurely from transportation (1834) and committing sacrilege or stealing a letter (1835). Then, in 1837, 21 capital offences were torn from the statute book, with a restricted use of the death penalty for the remaining 16, at the urging of the Commissioners following a direct request for help from the Home Secretary, Lord John Russell.[24] This left only two capital crimes for which death was inflicted: murder and treason.

Hanging in chains was abolished in 1834, the pillory in 1837 and in 1836 prisoners charged with felony were finally given the right to be fully represented by counsel. This followed numerous unsuccessful Bills in Parliament which were defeated by members of the House of Lords including judges until, again with the assistance of the Commissioners, a Bill introduced by William Ewart MP was passed by both houses as the Prisoners' Counsel Act. In the words of the Attorney-General, Sir John Campbell, "it was absolutely necessary to vindicate the law of England from a deep and disgraceful stain".[25]

With the aid of Romilly and the Criminal Law Commissioners the penal philosophy of Beccaria had finally triumphed over those of both Madan and Paley in England.

---

23. *Parliamentary Papers.* (1836) xxxvi. p. 183.
24. *Ibid.* (1837) xxxi. p. 1.
25. *Hansard.* 3rd series. (17 February 1836) vol. 31, col. 500.

CHAPTER 4

CRIMINAL LAW AND PUNISHMENTS

Torture and the death penalty have been dealt with in the preceding chapters since Beccaria saw them as the worst features of the criminal justice system in his day and because they remain so in many parts of the world today. Now, however, we will turn to consider the remainder of his work on issues that are also of great interest within the scope of penal law.

Reform of Criminal Justice

Beccaria's thesis is often referred to as a "little book" and although it does indeed contain only 42 brief chapters and sections this short treatise has had the remarkable and extensive impact on penal thinking already noted. Its influence in its day was revolutionary, and much of it is still relevant today. However, it should be remembered that the book was published over 200 years ago. Hence, although Beccaria's enlightened and humanist work transformed the law in ways from which we still benefit, nevertheless, as will be seen, it bears some hallmarks of its time, including in terms of style, that can puzzle the twenty-first century mind.

In a Preface to *On Crimes and Punishments*, the translator of the first English edition suggested that reducing the cruel penal laws to a standard of reason should be of interest to all mankind. Noting, eighteen months after its first publication, that it had penetrated to all parts of Europe, he claimed that it should be particularly acceptable to English people because of the eloquent and forcible manner in which the author pleaded the cause of liberty, benevolence and humanity.

"Perhaps", the translator continued, "no book, on any subject, was ever received with more avidity, more generally read, or more universally applauded". Some, he said, might think it useless in England, where from the excellence of the laws and government no cruelty or oppression could be found. He observed, however, that on the contrary there was a great deal still to be done to perfect our system of legislation. The examples of this that he gave included the confinement of debtors, the filth and horror of English prisons and the extortions by minor officers of justice. Moreover, he added, referring to the criminal law's "Bloody Code", the number of criminals put to death in England was much greater than in any other part of Europe.[1] This is, however, open to doubt.

In Beccaria's own introduction to the book he stresses the urgent need for reform of the criminal justice system to correct the errors and irregularities accumulated over centuries. A medieval spirit, he writes, still informs the criminal law. To enlighten those who from a mistaken love of liberty would introduce anarchy and those who would be glad to reduce their fellow-men to the uniform regularity of a convent he proposes to deal with the following questions, the first two of which we have already examined:

- Is death a penalty really *useful and necessary* for the security and good order of society?
- Are torture and torments *just* and do they attain the *end* which the law aims at?
- What will be the penalty suitable for particular crimes?
- What is the best way of preventing crimes?
- Are the same penalties equally useful in all times?
- What influence have they on customs?

These problems, he says, deserve to be solved with geometric precision to prevail over clouds of sophistication, seductive eloquence and timid doubt.

However, it is important we should note that he emphasises that his purpose is a frank search for truth not in order to diminish legitimate authority but to strengthen it. And, he also points out how few studies of the subject there have been and, after indicating that "the immortal President, Montesquieu" (as Beccaria calls the great humanist) had only lightly touched upon

---

1. Cesare Beccaria. (1775 – 4th edn) *An Essay on Crimes and Punishments with a Commentary by Mons. De Voltaire.* London, F. Newbery, pp. vii-viii and on the "bloody code" see John Hostettler (2009) *A History of Criminal Justice in England and Wales.* Hook: Waterside Press, pp. 113, 125, 175.

it, declares that, although not his equal, he will follow him and his influential work, *De L'esprit des Lois* (The Spirit of the Laws), in pleading the cause of humanity.[2] Nonetheless, he adds that the "thinking men, for whom I write, will be able to distinguish my steps from his".[3] I will consider myself fortunate, he says, if like him I can obtain the thanks of the disciples of reason and inspire them with that pleasing thrill of emotion with which sensitive minds respond to advocates who plead the cause of humanity.

Although Montesquieu said little about penal law he nevertheless opposed severe penalties for crimes and believed a light penalty could have as great a deterrent effect as more rigorous punishment. He sowed the seeds of a new penal philosophy with what was then a novel and imaginative belief that the purpose of the criminal law should be threefold, i.e. to:

(i) safeguard the liberty and security of the individual;
(ii) limit the power of the state in order to avoid despotism and arbitrary rule; and
(iii) ensure that punishments should always be moderate.

Under Montesquieu's influence two philosophical themes course through Beccaria's work. These are the social contract theory[4] and the principle of utility, or the greatest happiness divided among the greatest number, which, as we have seen, inspired his extraordinary follower Jeremy Bentham. Hence, he writes, each citizen sacrifices a part of his freedom to the protection of legal sanctions for the benefit of all.

Penal Law

Punishments are frequently described as being either retributive or utilitarian. Retribution, or vengeance, is commonly considered to give the criminal

---

2. J.A. Farrer. (1880) *Crimes and Punishments including a New Translation of Beccaria's Dei Delitti e Delle Pene.* London, Chatto and Windus, p. 119.
3. *Ibid.*
4. For Beccaria this meant the people surrendering only a minimum of their liberty to secure good laws and government unlike Rousseau's total surrender.

what he deserves. Its history goes back to Aristotle who believed that just retribution involved a proportional reprisal. In more modern times, James Fitzjames Stephen wrote that the primary object of legal punishment was, "the direct prevention of crime, either by fear, or by disabling or even destroying ... to gratify the public desire for vengeance upon such offenders as justify exemplary punishments."[5]

There was a great deal of public support in England and on the European continent for this approach in the eighteenth century but Beccaria decries such notions, which still remain widespread, as useless and unjust. The purpose of punishments, he writes, is not to torment and afflict a sensitive being or to undo a crime which has already been committed. Could, he asks, "a political body, which is a calm agent that moderates the passions of private individuals, harbour useless cruelty which is the tool of fury and fanaticism or of weak tyrants?" "Can the cries of a poor wretch", he continues, turn back time and undo actions which have already been done?"[6]

Utilitarians, on the other hand, believe in the deterrent value of punishment. In Beccaria's words the purpose of punishments is to prevent the offender from doing fresh harm to his fellows and to deter others from doing likewise. They should be selected to make the most effective and lasting impression on the minds of men with the least possible torment to the body of the condemned person.[7]

Political morality, says Beccaria, will provide no lasting advantage unless founded on the unwavering sentiments of mankind. And when a law deviates from these sentiments it will encounter a resistance that will ultimately prevail over it. No man ever voluntarily gave up a part of his liberty for the public good; that is a chimera which exists only in romances. Each of us would wish, if it were possible, that the rules which bind others should not bind ourselves. There are, he says, three sources of the moral and political principles which govern mankind, namely revelation, natural law, and social

---

5. J.F. Stephen. (1883) *A History of the Criminal Law of England.* London, Macmillan, vol. ii, p. 83.
6. David Young. (1986) *Beccaria: On Crimes and Punishments.* Indianapolis, Hackett Publishing Company. p. 23.
7. *Ibid.*

conventions, all three of which contribute to the happiness of this present mortal life.

There are, therefore, three distinct kinds of virtue and vice – the religious, the natural, and the political. These three kinds ought never to conflict although the consequences and duties that flow from any one of them do not necessarily flow from the others. The idea of political virtue is variable; that of natural virtue would always be clear and manifest but for the stupidity or passions of men; whilst the idea of religious virtue remains ever the same since it is revealed directly from God. But the prime purpose remains – *the greatest happiness divided among the greatest number.*[8]

The Origins of Punishments and the Right to Punish

Beccaria's Chapter 2 deals briefly with the origin of punishments. Men, he says, are by nature independent but unite together in society. Weary of living in a continual state of war, and enjoying a liberty of little value from the uncertainty of its duration, they sacrificed one part of it to enjoy the remainder in peace and security. The sum of all these portions of the liberty of each individual constitutes the sovereignty of a nation. And, this sovereignty has to be defended from usurpation which could plunge society into its former chaos. To this end punishments are established against those who would break the laws. Laws are required to counterbalance the effects of the passions of the individual who opposes the common good.

Neither the power of eloquence nor truths are sufficient to restrain, for any length of time, those passions which lead to crime.[9] The only effective restraint is punishment. This means giving up a number of rights although this does not include forfeiting the right to life. Hence the death penalty is impermissible quite apart from not producing the results claimed for it. At the same time Beccaria is adamant that punishments themselves have to be restrained and this is a crucial aspect of the book.

---

8. J.A. Farrer. *Crimes and Punishments including a new translation of Beccaria's Dei Delitti e Delle Pene. Op. cit.* pp. 113-4, 118.
9. Cesare Beccaria. *An Essay on Crimes and Punishments with a Commentary Attributed to Mons. De Voltaire. Op. cit* pp. 5-7.

Beccaria follows Montesquieu in declaring that every punishment which does not arise from absolute necessity is oppressive. Upon this principle the right to punish crimes is founded. Or, in other words, every act of authority of one man over another, for which there is no absolute necessity, is tyrannical.[10] Thus, it is necessary to defend the sacred public liberty entrusted to the care of the state from the encroachment of hostile individuals. But the punishment must be proportionate to the crime to preserve liberty and because no advantage in moral policy can be lasting unless founded upon "the indelible sentiments of the heart of man."

To Beccaria justice has nothing to do with physical power but means that bond which is necessary to keep the interests of individuals united. Without it men would return to a state of barbarity. What is crucial is that he sees all punishments which exceeded the necessity of preserving this bond as totally unjust. The punishment of crimes could only be determined by law and penal laws could be made only by the legislator who represents the whole of society united by the social contract. And, no judge or magistrate, under cover of the public good, should increase the punishment laid down by the law. Judges should not assume the role of legislators – a view strongly endorsed by Bentham who tended to regard all judges as venal.

Interpretation of the Law

Dealing with widespread judicial abuse on the European continent, Beccaria continues that the right to interpret penal laws cannot possibly be left with the criminal law judges, for the very reason that they are not legislators. They do not receive the laws from our ancestors as a family tradition, as a legacy that only left to posterity the duty of obeying them. They receive them from a living society, not as obligations arising from an ancient oath which would be null and void as binding men not then born.

The laws receive their force and authority from the tacit acceptance by citizens of the social contract, which requires the regulation of private interests harmful to the common good. Their interpretation does not fall to the

---

10. *Ibid.* p. 7.

judge whose sole function is to examine whether a prisoner has or has not committed an illegal act. In every criminal case the judge should reach a conclusion based on the general law and then determine acquittal or punishment.

Consequences

The first consequence of these principles is that only laws can decree punishments for crimes, and the only authority that can make penal laws is the legislator. No judge or magistrate then, as a member of society, can with justice inflict on any other member of society punishment that is not authorised by law. And he must not, by invoking the public good, increase a legal punishment. Of course, judges do in fact to some extent make law and they often have a discretion in regard to sentencing.

The second consequence, says Beccaria, is that if every individual is bound to society, society is equally bound to him by a contract which, from its nature, equally binds both parties. This obligation, which descends from the throne to the cabin, is in the interests of all and the conventions that are useful to the greatest number should be punctually observed. Violation of this contract by any individual can only lead to anarchy. The word "obligation", he adds, is one of those which is much more frequent in ethics than in any other science, and which is the abbreviated symbol of a train of reasoning rather than of a single idea. Seek for an idea corresponding to the word "obligation" and you will seek in vain. Reason about it, and you will both understand yourself and be understood by others.

The legislator, who represents society, can only make general laws to bind members and cannot judge whether any individual has broken the social contract and invited punishment. For in this case there are two parties, the legislator who insists there has been a violation of the contract and the person accused who denies it. There has to be a third party to decide this contest and that is a judge or magistrate from whose verdict, which should simply affirm or deny facts, there should be no appeal.

Thirdly, if it could be proved that the severity of punishments, even though not immediately contrary to the public good or to the prevention of crimes, is useless then such severity would be contrary to virtue and enlightened reason. Men should be governed in a state of freedom and happiness and not in a state of slavery based on cruelty. Such severity would also be contrary to justice and the nature of the social contract itself.

It would be unjust in that it would reduce men in the following ages to a herd of brutes with no power of judgment or action. The laws receive their force and authority from an oath of fidelity, either implied or expressed, which living subjects have sworn as part of the social contract in order to curb and regulate the disorders arising from private interests. This is the natural and real source of the authority of the laws.

Who, then, is the rightful interpreter of the laws? The sovereign, who is the trustee of the will of the people, or the judge whose sole function is to examine whether a man has committed an illegal act or not? In every criminal case a judge should reason logically. The statement of the general law should constitute the major premise, with the conformity or otherwise of the action with the law the minor premise. Acquittal or punishment should be the conclusion. If the judge feels obliged to interpret by what he sees as imperfections in the law, or if he chooses to do so, the door is open to uncertainty and this cannot be permitted.

Spirit of the Law

For judges and magistrates to take into account the "spirit of the laws", declares Beccaria, is dangerous and is not the important thing since it is like "breaking down a dam before the torrent of opinions".[11] Although, he says, this seems paradoxical to some, who are more concerned about a little present inconvenience than the pernicious but remote consequences which flow from a false principle, to Beccaria it is perfectly clear. He continues,

> Every man has his own point of view – a different one at different times; so that 'the spirit of the laws' would mean the result of good or bad logic on the part of the judge, of an easy or difficult digestion; it would depend now on the violence of his passions, now on the feebleness of the sufferer, on the relationship between the judge and the

---

11. J. A. Farrer. *Crimes and Punishments including a new translation of Beccaria's DeiDelitti e Delle Pene. Op. cit.* p. 127.

plaintiff, or on all those minute forces which change the appearances of everything in the fluctuating mind of man.[12]

The life and liberty of a defendant could be at the mercy of the false ideas or ill humour of a judge who mistakes the result of his own confused reasoning for a just interpretation of the law.

Hence we see, he says, the same crimes punished differently at different times in the same courts. This is the consequence of the judges adopting the instability of arbitrary interpretation instead of consulting the voice of the laws. Whilst rigorous observance of the letter of the penal law can be corrected by the legislature amending the law, interpretation by judges can lead to uncertainty and injustice. Once the law is fixed it should be observed literally with the judge determining simply whether an action is in breach of the law. Under a fixed code of laws citizens acquire that consciousness of personal security which is the object of social life and enables them to calculate exactly the evil consequences of an offence. No inconvenience that may arise from a strict observance of the letter of penal laws is to be compared with the undesirability of subjecting them to judicial interpretation.

In this regard Beccaria is being too legalistic as the spirit of the law is indeed important. In England at least, jury nullification over the centuries has frequently softened harsh laws in a manner that Beccaria surely would have applauded. "Perverse verdicts", as they were often called, meant, and still mean, the jury's power to acquit a defendant on the basis of conscience even when, on the evidence and law, he or she would be technically guilty. Law Lord, Lord Devlin (writing when Sir Patrick Devlin), noted that they are a protection against laws that the ordinary man might regard as "harsh and oppressive" and an insurance "that the criminal law will conform to the ordinary man's idea of what is fair and just."[13]

Recent modern cases in Britain that come to mind include acquittals in trials for alleged criminal damage to jet aircraft by anti-war and environmental campaigners where juries have ignored directions from the bench. In one such trial, in 1996, four women were acquitted of damaging

---

12. J. A. Farrer. *Ibid.* pp. 127-8.
13. Sir Patrick Devlin. (1966) *Trial by Jury*. London, Methuen & Co., p. 160.

a British Aerospace Hawk jet in protest against the sale of such jets to foreign countries.[14]

Another instance was the trial of Clive Ponting in 1985. He was a senior civil servant in the Ministry of Defence who was tried under section 2(1) of the Official Secrets Act 1911 for leaking classified documents to a Member of Parliament. His defence centred on the argument that the disclosure was permitted by the statute if it was "in the interests of the state". However, the judge held that the "interests of state" were not for the jury to decide. No proof of *mens rea* (an evil intention or knowledge that an act was wrong) beyond an intention to commit the act was necessary. Nonetheless, apparently following their consciences, the jury acquitted Ponting.[15]

As the jurist and judge, James Fitzjames Stephen, perceptively wrote, "Though the judges are, and are known to be, independent of the executive government, it is naturally felt that their sympathies are likely to be on the side of authority. The public at large feel more sympathy with jurymen than they do with judges, and accept their verdicts with much less hesitation and distrust."[16]

Beccaria believes that the true test of crimes is the injury done to society and not the intention of the perpetrator. Those who think that the criminal's intention is the true measure of crimes are wrong. For intention depends upon the actual impression of things upon a man and on his mental disposition, things which vary in all men according to their ideas passions and circumstances. It would therefore be necessary to form a fresh law for every crime. However, here Beccaria is in danger of missing the point that under the rule of law evil intention (*mens rea*) is an essential ingredient of most crimes which must be tested by intention and not by the consequences of the crime. Otherwise individuals with no intention of committing a crime may be caught up in the consequences of one and found guilty.

---

14. *Financial Times.* (6 August 1966).
15. *R. v. Ponting.* (1985) Central Criminal Court.
16. J.F. Stephen. (1877) "Suggestions for the Reform of the Criminal Law". *Nineteenth Century.* London, Sampson, Low, Marston & Co., vol. i. p. 574.

Obscurity of the Law

If the interpretation of laws by judges is an evil, says Beccaria, it is clear that their obscurity, which necessarily involves interpretation, must also be so. The mischief caused is even greater if the laws are written in language that is not understood by men and women not versed in the law. In that case the people, being unable to judge how the laws affect their lives and liberty, become dependent on a small number of men who interpret the laws which instead of being public and general are rendered private and particular. That, indeed, is the established custom in the greater part of our "cultivated and enlightened Europe".

Crimes will be less frequent as the laws are more universally read and understood since the eloquence of the passions is greatly assisted by the ignorance and uncertainty of punishments. Hence it follows that without written laws no society will ever acquire a fixed form of government where power is vested in the whole and not in a mere part of society, and where laws are changed only by the will of the people, uncorrupted by the pressure of private interests. Experience and reason have taught us that the probability and certainty of human traditions diminish in proportion to their distance from their source. So that if there is no standing memorial of the social contract, how will laws ever resist the inevitable force of time and passion?

From this, Beccaria continues, we see how useful is the art of printing which makes the public, and not a few individuals, the guardians and defenders of the law. It is this art, which by publishing literature, has gradually dissipated the gloomy spirit of plot and intrigue before the advance of knowledge and science. This is why we see in Europe the diminution of those atrocious crimes that afflicted our ancestors and rendered them by turns tyrants or slaves. Those who know the history of two or three centuries ago as well of our own century, can see that from the lap of luxury have sprung the most tender virtues of humanity, charity and the toleration of human errors. They will know what has resulted from that which is so wrongly called "old-fashioned simplicity and honesty". Humanity groaning under revengeful superstition, the greed and ambition of a few staining with human blood the thrones and palaces of kings; secret assassinations and public massacres; "every noble a tyrant to the people and the ministers of the gospel polluting with blood hands that every day came into contact with of the God of mercy". These are not the works of the present enlightened age which some, however, call corrupt.[17]

The Division of Punishments

According to Beccaria, some crimes tend directly to the destruction of society, others affect individual citizens by placing in peril their lives, their property or their honour. Others, again, are actions contrary to the laws which relate to the general good of the community. Any action which is not included in the above three categories can only be called a crime, or punished as such, by those whose interests are affected by it. The consequent uncertainty has produced in some nations a system of ethics contrary to the laws and has produced many actual codes of laws at total variance with one another as well as a number of laws with unreasonably severe penalties. As a result the words *virtue* and *vice* have assumed a vague and variable meaning leading to apathy among communities.

The opinion that each citizen should have liberty to do anything that is not illegal is a political precept which should be defended by the laws, given effect by the magistrates and be believed in by the people. Without it there can be no lawful society. It is a just recompense for our sacrifice of that universal liberty of action which is common to all and is only limited by our natural powers. By this principle our minds become free, active and vigorous. By this alone we are inspired with that virtue which knows no fear, and not with that flexible kind which is only worthy of a man who can put up with a precarious and uncertain existence.

A study of the laws of different nations is considered by Beccaria almost always to show that the concepts of *virtue* and *vice* and of *good citizen* and *criminal* change in the course of time. Not in accordance with changes in the circumstances of a country and the general interest but according to the views and errors of different legislators. Often the views of one age form the

---

17. J.A. Farrer. *Crimes and Punishments including a new translation of Beccaria's Dei Delitti e Delle Pene. Op. cit.* pp. 131-32.

basis of the morality of later ones. Strong passions, the offspring of fanaticism and enthusiasm are weakened by time and little by little become the prudence of the age and a useful instrument in the hands of a strong man. Attempts against the life and liberty of a citizen are crimes of the highest nature. Not only assassinations and robberies committed by the people but those committed by aristocrats and judges. Their example has a more powerful effect and destroys the ideas of justice in the community, and substitutes the right of the strongest which is equally dangerous to those who exercise it as to those who suffer from it.

Crimes of High Treason

Treason has always been the most political of all crimes with penalties terrible to contemplate, both in continental Europe and Britain. In Europe men were torn apart whilst in England a man, as we have seen, was hanged, drawn and quartered whilst women, on the other hand, were burnt at the stake after being tarred.

In its general sense, the crime of treason consists in the violation of the allegiance due from the subject to the sovereign as supreme head of state. It might appear that to define this in legal terms would present little difficulty. Indeed, because treason is regarded as the most serious offence in the calendar of crimes it was one of the first crimes to be defined by statute in England in the Middle Ages. That was the Statute of Treasons of 1352 (25 Edw. III st. 5). However, although the Act was relatively narrow in its scope, over the centuries the courts extended the meaning of treason by the doctrine of constructive treason to incorporate a whole number of acts, such as pulling down brothels by apprentices or combining to improve wages by workmen as treason in endeavouring to destroy the king.

High treason is considered by Beccaria to be the worst of crimes because it is most injurious to society. Nevertheless, much the same as happened in England with constructive treasons must have occurred on the continent, since he asserts that tyranny and ignorance have clouded the clearest ideas and given this name of treason to crimes of a different nature with the same punishment for each. As a consequence, in thousands of cases men have been sacrificed as victims to a word. Every crime, even of the most private nature, injures society. But not every crime threatens its immediate destruction. Moral as well as physical actions have their limited sphere of activity and are differently embraced, like all the movements of nature, by time and space. Hence, only a misleading interpretation, which is generally the philosophy of slavery, can confound what eternal truth has distinguished by unchangeable differences.

Voltaire

Not surprisingly, Voltaire was also opposed to constructive treasons. As he saw it high treason was an offence against the security of the commonwealth or of the king its representative. It was considered to be parricide and therefore should not have been extended to offences that bore no analogy to that crime. In making it high treason to commit a theft in a house belonging to the state, or even to speak seditious words, lessened the horror which the crime of high treason should inspire. In ideas of great crimes there should be nothing arbitrary. If a theft from a father was considered as parricide the bond of filial piety was broken and the son would regard his parent as a terrible monster. Indeed, every exaggeration in law tended to the law's destruction.

In common crimes, continued Voltaire, the laws of England were favourable to the accused. But in cases of high treason they were against him. The notorious Titus Oates and another man deposed that fifty Jesuits had conspired to assassinate Charles II and that they had seen commissions for the officers who were to command an army of rebels. This was sufficient to authorize the tearing out of the hearts of several people and dashing them in their faces. This should not be allowed to happen when those deposing are notorious villains and that to which they deposed was improbable.

Personal Security

Then come crimes against the personal security of individuals. Beccaria believes this security is the primary aim of decent society and thus its breach justifies serious punishments. Hence injuries to a man's person should be punished by corporal punishments. Under this head, he insists, also fall not only killings and thefts by the common people but also those committed by noblemen and magistrates whose influence and force are greater and destroy in those subject to them all ideas of justice and duty. Neither the noble nor the rich man should be able to pay a price for injuries committed against the feeble and the poor.

Nor should riches, which when protected by law are the prize of industry, be allowed to sustain tyranny. Whenever the law permits a man to cease to be a person and become a thing there is no liberty. This is the magic secret that changes citizens into beasts of burden and forms the chain with which the tyrant fetters the actions of the weak and imprudent. It is the reason why in some governments, that have all the semblance of liberty, tyranny lies hidden, gains strength and grows. Men build the strongest barriers against open tyranny but fail to see the invisible insect which gnaws them away.

Of what kind then, asks Beccaria, will be the punishments due to the crimes of noblemen whose privileges form so great a part of the laws in all countries? In practice, of course, the nobles are often able to avoid punishment altogether. But without entering into controversy about inequality Beccaria comes down firmly for punishments being the same for the greatest citizen as for the least. There should be no opportunity allowed for special treatment otherwise some people would have no fear of the law.

Despite England's "Bloody Code", he says, its rulers do not rule by terror alone. Mercy could be shown by royal pardon but the philosophy and ideology of the law means that rich and poor alike could be sent to the gallows.[18] And, if anyone should say that the same punishment inflicted upon a nobleman and upon a commoner is not really the same because of the differences in their education, and the disgrace spread over an illustrious family, Beccaria replies that the sensibility of the criminal is not the measure of punishment, it is the public injury. And that is all the greater when committed by the more highly placed man.

---

18. See Douglas Hay.(1975) *Albion's Fatal Tree: Crime and Society in Eighteenth Century England.* London, Allen Lane, Penguin Books Ltd.

The Purpose of Punishment

Fundamental to the purpose of punishment in Beccaria's eyes is the need to ensure the continued existence of society. To that end, as we have seen, for Beccaria punishments do not exist to torment human beings or to rescind a crime already committed. They are to prevent criminals from doing further harm to society and to deter others from committing crimes. Can a political body, he asks, authorise the torments and useless cruelty that are the instruments of furious fanaticism or the impotence of tyrants? Far from being influenced by passion such a body should be the calm moderator of the passions of individuals. Could the groans of a tortured prisoner call back the past or reverse the crime? The sole end of punishment, therefore, is not only to prevent the criminal from doing further injury to society but also to prevent others from committing a similar offence. In other words, general and individual deterrence. Hence, again as already noted, he believes that punishments, and the means of inflicting them, should be those that make the strongest and most lasting impressions on the mind of the criminal with the least torment to his body.

Prompt Punishment

In England in Beccaria's day, following a proposal by Henry Fielding, the Murder Act of 1752[19] had, as a means of terror, blatantly given judges a discretion to have persons convicted of murder executed and their corpses hung publicly in a gibbet all within 48 hours of the sentence.[20] Fielding believed execution so close to conviction would help spectators reflect upon the horror of the crime instead of feeling pity for the criminal.

The first offender to be executed in accordance with the statute was Thomas Wilford who "was taken from the bar weeping and in great agonies, lamenting his sad fate."[21] Of course, the punishment was irreversible and if

---

19. 25 Geo. 2, c. 37.
20. John Hostettler. (1994) *The Politics of Punishment.* Chichester, Barry Rose Law Publishers, p. 97.
21. *The London Magazine.* (1752) vol. 21. pp. 333-4.

the conviction was founded on mistake or perjury there was little time for this to be brought to light and the execution halted. As a consequence, the progressive English Criminal Law Commissioners appointed in 1833 publicly advised the government that a greater time between a conviction and execution should be allowed and that this would greatly overbalance any benefit arising to society from the terror supposed to be inspired by a speedy execution which they seriously doubted anyway.[22]

However, Beccaria's view, like Fielding's, is that the more immediately after the commission of a crime a punishment is inflicted the more just and useful it will be. More just, he argues with special pleading and his normal humanism forsaking him, because a criminal is spared those useless and fierce torments of suspense which are greater in a person of vigorous imagination and because the absence of liberty is in itself a punishment and should precede the sentence by the shortest possible period. Imprisonment, therefore, is simply the safe custody of a citizen pending the finding of his guilt and, being disagreeable, should be as brief and easy as possible.

The shortness of the time should be determined by the necessary preparations for the trial and the right of priority of the older prisoners. And, the strictness of the confinement should be no more than is necessary for the prevention of escape or the concealment of the proofs of the crime. The trial itself should be finished in the shortest possible time. What contrast, he asks, is more cruel than that between a judge's ease and a defendant's anguish? In general the punishment should be as efficient as possible for the restraint of others and to give the least possible pain to the prisoner.

Public Tranquility

There are crimes that disturb the public peace and civic tranquillity. They include, maintains Beccaria, noise and riots in the public streets, which were made for the convenience of people and traffic, and fanatical sermons that excite the passions of the crowds. There was a long history of such "crimes" in history going back to the fanaticism of the sermons of Savanarola in the

---

22. Second Report. Parl. Papers (1836) xxxvi. p. 183.

fifteenth century. These passions, says Beccaria, gather strength from the number of hearers who, though deaf to calm and solid reasoning, are always affected by obscure and mysterious enthusiasm. The illumination of a city at night at the public expense, guards stationed in various quarters of the city, simple moral discourses on religion in churches and speeches in national assemblies and parliaments – all these are effective means for preventing the dangerous effects of the misguided passions of the people. These should be the principal objects of the vigilance of the magistrate, which the French call police, but if this magistrate should act in an arbitrary manner, and not in accordance with the law, he opens a door to tyranny which always surrounds the boundaries of political liberty.

There is no exception to the general axiom that "every citizen ought to know when his actions are guilty or innocent". If censors, and arbitrary magistrates in general, are considered necessary in any government, this proceeds from a weakness in its constitution and is foreign to the nature of a well-organized government. More victims have been sacrificed to obscure tyranny by the uncertainty of their lot than by public and formal cruelty since the latter revolts men's minds more than it debases them. The true tyrant always begins by mastering opinion, the precursor of courage for the latter can only show itself in the clear light of truth, in the fire of passion, or in ignorance of danger.

Pleas of the Crown and Confessions

In the early history of criminal law in England[23], in place of savage vigilante vengeance, Saxon dooms provided for compensation to be paid to a person or his family if he were injured or killed during the commission of a crime. In a sense it was an early form of restorative justice. There was also a fine payable to the king, known as a *wite*. This was an innovation and, with later additions, was to feed the wealth, and the growth of royal power for centuries to come. It saw the beginning of the encroachment of political

---

23. See John Hostettler. (2009) *A History of Criminal Justice in England and Wales.* Hook: Waterside Press, chapters 1-4.

considerations into the arena of criminal justice with the Crown exerting more and more control.

Enforcing the law proved difficult, however, and that in turn led to the gradual emergence of the concept of serious crimes such as murder being in breach of the king's peace. In consequence, as the power of the kings grew, prosecutions began to be conducted in his name as a means of acquiring income for the Crown. Sensing an easy means of raising large revenues, the Norman and Angevin kings proceeded to make the king's peace permanent and universal throughout England. Whatever the punishment for a crime, and it was usually death, it was accompanied by a fine or seizure of property to go to the royal coffers. Hence criminal cases came to be headed *Rex v. A.B.* as indictments still are today.

A similar situation existed in Europe which Beccaria deals with under the heading "Of the Treasury". There was a time, he says, when nearly all penalties were financial. Men's crimes fed the expectations of the ruler. Attempts against the public safety are an object of gain and he whose function it is to preserve the peace finds his interest in seeing it attacked. The object of punishment becomes a suit between the monarch's treasury, which collects the penalty, and the criminal.

It also confers other rights on the treasury and inflicts new grievances on the offender. The judge becomes an advocate of the Crown instead of an impartial investigator of the truth, an agent for the Chancellor of the Exchequer instead of the guardian and minister of the law. Hence, the system of confession to a crime in order to augment the ruler's finances became the central point of all criminal procedure. In his day Beccaria says that without such a confession a criminal proved guilty by evidence incurs a penalty lower than the one legally justified by his crime. And without it he also escapes torture for other crimes of the same kind which he may have committed.

With a confession, on the other hand, the judge becomes master of the criminal and tortures him to get from him as much profit as he can. Once the crime is established confession is made a convincing means of proof that it was committed by the prisoner. Such a confession extracted by the agonies and despair of physical pain is alone regarded as proof of guilt. At the same time, a confession that is made without the overpowering fears of a trial by torture is held insufficient for a verdict of guilty. Inquiries and proofs which throw light on the case but weaken the claims of the treasury are excluded. The judge becomes the enemy of the accused, who stands in chains before him, the prey of misery of torments, and the most terrible future. He does not seek to find the truth but to entrap the prisoner and prove his own infallibility.

The evidence that justifies a man's imprisonment rests with the judge. In order that a man may prove himself innocent he had first to be declared guilty. This, says Beccaria, is called an *offensive prosecution* and such were criminal proceedings in nearly every part of "enlightened" Europe in the eighteenth century. What a complex maze of strange absurdities, he declares, doubtless incredible to a more fortunate posterity! Only the philosophers of the future will be able to find, by searching in the nature of man, that such a system actually existed.

Today, in England confessions are treated with reserve and require back-up evidence. How they were regarded and treated on the continent in Beccaria's time is searingly revealed in his book and outlined here in this chapter.

CHAPTER 5

CRIMES DIFFICULT TO PROVE AND OTHERS

In the chapter of his book under the heading of 'Crimes Difficult to Prove' Beccaria deals, among other things, with adultery, homosexuality, infanticide and suicide. In his day society believed these to be serious crimes. Indeed, in some societies they still are considered to be so and even in Britain, except for adultery, they have only recently been released from that stigma. In Beccaria's time they produced not only severe punishments but disgrace and ostracism from society. As with other crimes on the European continent proof often consisted in confessions extracted by torture and this was generally accepted by the public. So heinous were these so-called crimes represented to be that Beccaria's views were unusually forward-looking and seeing them with a new eye publicly and without fear (although with some circumspection) took a great deal of courage.

Presumptions

Beccaria considers that reason rarely plays a part in the drafting of a nation's laws. As a consequence the weakest and most unclear evidence, and even assumptions, are frequently thought sufficient proof of the most atrocious, obscure and fanciful (and therefore most improbable) crimes. It is as though the law and the judge need not inquire into the truth but merely accept that the crime is proved. As though there is not a greater risk of condemning an innocent person when the probability of his guilt is lower.

There are some crimes which, though they occur frequently, are difficult to prove. Where this is so the difficulty of producing evidence suggests the likelihood of innocence. In these cases their frequency does not arise so much from their immunity as from other causes. The danger of their not being punished is of less importance and, therefore, the time for examination and prosecution should be diminished. This is different from what is usually done when crimes which are proved with the greatest difficulty, such as adultery and homosexuality, are "proved" with presumptions and half-proofs as if a man could be half innocent and half guilty as well as half punishable. It is in these cases that torture is used on the body of the accused, witnesses and even members of his family, with the indifference to its evil as some experts in Roman-canonical law who dictate laws to nations have advocated.

Adultery

Adultery is, of course, not a crime in modern society but the Church held it to be so in medieval times and that continued to be the case in continental Europe in Beccaria's day. Adultery he believes to be a crime, which considered politically, owes its existence to two causes, namely, the variable laws in force in society and the powerful attraction between the sexes. This attraction is similar in many ways to gravity and the springs of motion in the universe. In a like manner these are both diminished by distance. But they differ in one respect, the force of gravity decreases in proportion to the obstacles that oppose it whereas the sexual attraction gathers strength and vigour as the obstacles increase. Here probably Beccaria was relating to his own experience with the opposition of his father to his love affair with Teresa di Blasco.

If he were speaking to nations guided only by the laws of nature and without religion, he continued, he would tell them that there is a considerable difference between adultery and all other crimes. Adultery arises from an abuse of the universal necessity in human nature whereas all other crimes tend to the destruction of society and arise from momentary passions and not from a natural necessity. Those who have studied history and mankind consider that this need seems to be constant in all climates. If this is true all laws and customs are useless that attempt to diminish its effects. Such laws can only burden one part of society with the needs of the other part. Instead, those laws would be wise which, following the natural course of the river, would divide the stream into a number of equal branches and thus prevent flooding.

Conjugal fidelity is always greater in proportion as marriages are more numerous and less difficult. But when the pride of families, or parental authority, unite the sexes in place of the inclination of the parties, gallantry soon breaks the slender ties in spite of common moralists who exclaim against the effect whilst they pardon the cause. The act of adultery is so instantaneous, so mysterious and so concealed by the veil which the laws themselves have woven that it would be much easier to prevent it than punish it as a crime when it has been committed. For every crime which remains unpunished the punishment is an incentive. Such is the nature of the human mind that difficulties, if not insurmountable, embellish the object and spur us on to the pursuit. The mind, in Beccaria's view, naturally inclines to what is most agreeable and studiously avoids every idea that might create disgust.

Homosexuality

Homosexuality has also had a long history as a crime going back to ancient times and religions. Beccaria deals with it only briefly, no doubt in this case, inhibited by the strong aversion surrounding it in his day. He sees that although it is severely punished by the law, and so readily subjected to the tortures that triumph over innocence, it is founded less on the necessities of man, when living in a state of isolation and freedom, than on his passions when living in a state of society and slavery. It arises not so much from the satisfaction of pleasures as from teachings now in vogue that make men useless to themselves in order that they may be useful to others. In those educational establishments where young men are excluded from contact with the opposite sex their natural vigour is expended in unproductive activity.

Infanticide

Similarly, to Beccaria, infanticide is the effect of a cruel dilemma in which a woman who has succumbed to weakness or to violence against herself, finds herself. The alternative is either her own disgrace or the death of a being unable to feel the loss of life. How can she avoid preferring the latter to the inevitable misery of herself and her unhappy infant. The best method of preventing this crime, he says, would be to give efficient legal protection to the weak from the tyranny that exaggerates all vices that cannot be concealed under a cloak of virtue. He does not contend that it should cease to be a crime.

Suicide

Suicide was another act considered a crime in the eighteenth century, and indeed into the twentieth century. Beccaria thinks of it as a crime which seems not to allow of punishment since it can be inflicted only upon either the innocent or a dead body. In the first case it is unjust and tyrannical as the victim has not committed a crime. In the second case it has no more effect as an example than inflicting violence on a statue. Men love life too well to believe that the crime could ever be common from the difficulty of punishing it. Laws are obeyed from fear of punishment but death destroys all feelings of sensibility. What motive then could restrain the desperate hand of suicide?

He who kills himself does less injury to society than he who leaves his country for good since he leaves his property behind him whereas the emigrant takes with him at least part of what he owns. Besides, as the strength of a society consists in the number of citizens, he who quits one nation to reside in another sustains a double loss. One questions, therefore, whether it is advantageous to society for its members to emigrate. No law should be enacted that is not backed by force or is ineffectual. Opinion obeys the impressions of law unless they are applied with violence. And useless laws are regarded as obstacles to be overcome rather than as safeguards of the public good. Further, as our impressions are limited, enforcing the observance of useless laws can only destroy the influence of good laws. It is pointless to turn a state into a prison.

Once it is committed this crime of suicide cannot be punished. And to punish it beforehand would be to punish the intention, which is free from the power of human laws, and not the action. Punishment after death by suicide is in the hands of God alone. In regard to men it is not a crime because the punishment would fall on an innocent family. If it is suggested that such a punishment might prevent a crime, Beccaria answered that he who could calmly renounce the pleasures of life and accept the idea of eternal misery would never be influenced by the less powerful considerations of family and children.

In conclusion, Beccaria says that he does not wish to belittle the revulsion these crimes cause but wants to discover the sources from which they spring. The punishment of a crime could not be necessary or just, he says, if the laws have not endeavoured to prevent it by the best means which the times and circumstances will allow.

Voltaire on Suicide

In his Commentary on Beccaria's book, Voltaire indicated that in Roman law suicide was not forbidden and that a suicide's heirs could properly inherit on his death. In Beccaria's day, on the contrary, it was ordained that a stake be driven through the corpse of a suicide and every effort was made to dishonour his family. "We punish", he wrote, "a son for having lost a father, and a widow because she is deprived of her husband. We even confiscate the effects of the deceased, and rob the living of that which is justly their due. This custom, with many others, was derived from our canon law, which denies Christian burial to those who are guilty of suicide, concluding thence, that it is not lawful to inherit on earth from one who hath himself no inheritance in heaven." The canon law, he concluded, assures us that Judas Iscariot committed a greater crime in hanging himself than in betraying Jesus Christ.[1]

Smuggling

To Beccaria this is a real crime against the government and the nation but its punishment should not involve disgrace because its commission incurs

---

1. Cesare Beccaria. (1775) *An Essay on Crimes and Punishments with a Commentary by Mons. De Voltaire*. London, F Newbery, p. lxv.

no censure at the bar of public opinion. Offences which men do not consider can be committed against themselves do not interest them enough to produce public indignation against the offender. By inflicting heavy punishments for crimes that are not regarded as dishonourable we destroy the feeling for those that are. If the same punishment is imposed for killing a pheasant as for killing a man, or for forgery, all distinction between those crimes will vanish. In this way moral sentiments are destroyed in the heart of man. Sentiments that that have come about over many centuries and after much bloodshed. Sentiments that have flowered so slowly and with great difficulty, and for the establishment of which such sublime motives and solemn ceremonial were believed necessary.

Moreover, this crime arises from the laws themselves for the higher the customs duties the greater is the advantage to be gained and, consequently, the greater the temptation. The seizure of goods attempted to be smuggled is just but it would be better to reduce the duty since men take risks only in proportion to the gain expected. As this crime involves a theft of what belongs to the nation why, asked Beccaria, should it not bring disgrace to its perpetrators? The answer is that offences which people do not consider bring bad consequences to themselves personally do not interest them sufficiently to arouse their indignation. Generally mankind, upon whom remote consequences make little impression, do not see the evil that may result from the practice of smuggling especially if they enjoy a present advantage from it. They only perceive the loss suffered by the country. As a consequence they have some esteem for the smuggler and ignore his crimes by which they might suffer. They interest themselves only in those evils with which they are acquainted.

Should this crime then, committed by one who has nothing to lose, go unpunished? The answer is in the negative. There are certain types of smuggling which so affect the country's revenue that they deserve imprisonment. Nevertheless, the penalty has to be proportionate to the crime. For example, it would be highly unjust that a smuggler of tobacco should suffer the same punishment as a robber or assassin. But it would be fair if he were made to work in the nation's excise service which he had intended to defraud.

Bankruptcy

The requirement of good faith in contracts and the security of commerce compels the legislature to seek the imprisonment of bankrupts. It is necessary, however, to distinguish between the fraudulent and the honest bankrupt. The fraudulent bankrupt should be punished in the same manner as a fraudulent coiner for to falsify a coin, which is a pledge of the mutual obligations between citizens, is not a greater crime than to falsify those obligations themselves.

But it is different for the honest bankrupt who, after strict examination before professional judges, has proved that either the fraud, or losses of others, or misfortunes unavoidable by prudence, has stripped him of his goods. In this case upon what barbarous pretence should he be thrown into prison and deprived of his liberty? Why should he suffer the agonies of the really guilty and in despair be compelled to recant of his honesty? Conscious of his innocence he lives happily under the protection of those laws which, it is true, he has broken but not intentionally. Laws dictated by the greed of the rich, are accepted by the poor who are seduced by that universal and flattering hope which makes men believe that all unlucky accidents are the lot of others and only the most fortunate ones are theirs. Nonetheless, when men are subjected to laws they wish them to be as harsh as possible because the fear of being injured by others is always greater than their desire to inflict injuries themselves.

To return to the innocent bankrupt. His debt should not be cancelled until he has repaid his creditors in full. And until he has made total repayment he should not be allowed to leave the country without the consent of his creditors or work abroad unless the produce of such work should be for the benefit of his creditors? However, what pretence could justify depriving an innocent and unfortunate man of his liberty without the least benefit to his creditors. Some would say that the hardships of confinement would induce him to admit to fraud which is hardly likely if his examination has been thorough. It is a maxim of government that the disadvantages of the impunity of a crime are in direct proportion to the harm done to the public and in inverse proportion to the likelihood of its being proved.

It is also necessary to distinguish fraud with aggravating circumstances from simple fraud and that from perfect innocence. For the first, the punishment should be the same as for forgery. For the second, a lesser punishment but with possible loss of personal liberty. For the perfectly honest, the bankrupt should be allowed himself to choose the method of satisfying his creditors provided that if he has not been strictly honest the method can be decided by those creditors. And these distinctions should be fixed by law and not by the arbitrary and dangerous discretion of judges.

In a footnote Beccaria writes that it might be alleged that the interests of commerce and property must be secured. But commerce and property, he says, are not the end of the social contract but the means of obtaining that end. To expose all the members of society to cruel laws, in order to preserve them from evils necessarily caused by the infinite combinations which result from the actual state of political societies, would be to make the end subservient to the means. "In the former editions of this work", he claimed, "I myself fell into this error when I said that the honest bankrupt should be kept in custody as a pledge for his debts, or employed as a slave to work for his creditors. I am ashamed of having adopted so cruel an opinion. I have been accused of impiety; I did not deserve it. I have been accused of sedition; I deserved it as little. But I insulted all the rights of humanity, and was never reproached."[2]

This reference to slavery is a reminder that Beccaria lived in the eighteenth century and some of his theories are obsolete. Whilst he could not break out of all the prejudices of his time, what is so amazing is his humanity and his breathtaking attack on the then existing evils of European penal law.

Leading Questions

In England today leading questions by counsel are generally permitted in cross-examination but not in examination-in-chief. In eighteenth century Europe the law did not allow leading questions at all in a criminal trial. In

---

2. C. Beccaria. *An Essay on Crimes and Punishments with a Commentary by Monsieur Voltaire. Op. cit.* pp. 145-6.

other words, they are questions that suggest to the witness what the answer should be. Facts should therefore be approached indirectly. But whatever the reason for this the law had fallen into a serious contradiction in condemning such questions whilst authorising torture. Could there be a question, asks Beccaria, more suggestive than pain. Torture will suggest to a strong man an obstinate silence so that his punishment will be less extreme, whilst to a feeble man it will suggest confession to relieve him from present torment which affects him more than the apprehension of pain that is to come. If a special interrogation is contrary to natural rights, because it obliges a man to accuse himself, torture would certainly do that more effectively. Those who remain silent should be punished so that criminals, by their silence, may not evade justice. But this ignores the importance of the right to silence that existed in England in Beccaria's day, although it has lately been modified.[3] He does accept, however, that punishment would not be necessary where guilt is undeniable because in that case questioning is useless as would be a confession when there are sufficient proofs without it. This last case was most common as experience shows that in the greatest number of criminal prosecutions, the accused tends to plead not guilty.

Oaths

In criminal courts all witnesses were required to take an oath before giving evidence, a rule now changed in England so that a witness may affirm instead. In his time Beccaria saw oaths as causing a contradiction between the laws and natural feelings. They require an accused person to say he is a truthful man when it is in his interest to be false. As if a man can really swear to contribute to his own destruction, or as if religion would not be silent with most men when their interest speaks on the other side. The experience of all history shows that men have abused religion more than any other of "the

---

3. In England the right to silence was for centuries regarded as a basic right so that no one should have to convict himself or herself with their own words. This was diluted by the Criminal Justice and Public Order Act of 1994 which permits a court to draw inferences when an accused person does not mention something when charged or in his or her defence which they then seek to rely upon in court.

precious gifts of heaven". And why should criminals respect it when even the wisest of men have often violated it?

For the majority of people the motives which religion opposes to the tumult of fear and the love of life are too weak, because they are too far removed from the senses. The affairs of Heaven, declares Beccaria, are conducted by laws absolutely different from those which govern human affairs; so why confuse the one with the other? Why place men in the terrible dilemma of either sinning against God or concurring in their own ruin? The law, in fact, which enforces such an oath commands a man either to be a bad Christian or to be a martyr. The oath becomes gradually a mere formality, thus destroying the force of religious feelings, which for the majority of men are the only pledge of their honesty.

How useless oaths are, he suggests, is shown by experience. Every judge would bear him out when he says that no oath has ever yet made any criminal speak the truth. And reason confirms this. It declares that all laws are useless, and consequently injurious, if they are opposed to natural sentiments. Such laws incur the same fate as dams placed directly in the main stream of a river. Either they are immediately overwhelmed or they form a whirlpool which gradually corrodes and undermines them. However, he does not suggest affirmation or any other alternative and presumably believes evidence should just be given straight.

Sanctuaries

In medieval times sanctuaries were churches or other consecrated places where criminals could stay and avoid arrest and trial since neither the civil nor criminal process of the law could be executed there. They were abolished in England by statute in the reign of James I[4] but still existed on the continent in Beccaria's day. On this topic Beccaria raises two questions. The first is whether sanctuaries are just and, secondly, whether a convention between nations mutually to give up and extradite their criminals is useful? His reply starts from the premise that in no country should there be any

---

4. 21 Jac. 1, c. 28, s. 7.

place independent of, and above, the law. The power of the law should follow every citizen as the shadow follows the body. Sanctuaries and impunity differ only in degree. As the effective influence of punishments depends more on their certainty than their harshness men are more strongly seduced into crime by sanctuaries than they are deterred by punishment. To increase the number of sanctuaries is to create petty sovereign states since where the law has no power new "laws" will be formed that act contrary to the spirit of the state and society.

Extradition

As for extradition, some people, he continues, maintain that in whatever country a crime is committed the criminal may be justly punished for it in any other country. It is as if a man could live in one country and be subject to the laws of another even when the respective laws were contradictory. They think that an act committed in Constantinople might be punished in Paris for the abstract reason that he who offends humanity should have enemies throughout mankind and be the object of universal hatred. As if judges were the knights errant of human nature in general rather than guardians of particular conventions between men. The place of punishment should be where the crime is committed as that is where the necessity of punishing an individual for the general good lies. A villain who has not broken the laws of a society of which he is not a member may be feared, and for that reason be expelled and exiled by that society. But he cannot be legally and formally punished there since it is for the law to avenge not the intrinsic value of particular actions but the breach of the law.

Whether international extradition is useful or not Beccaria declines to say until there are laws better suited to human needs and human rights. That is until there are milder punishments and the abolition of arbitrary power.

CHAPTER 6

VARIOUS TOPICS AND IMPRISONMENT

Prosecutions and Prescriptions

As soon as *prima facie* proofs of a crime and its reality are fully confirmed, says Beccaria, the criminal must be allowed time and opportunity for his defence. Yet, the time allowed must be so short as not to interfere with the speed of his punishment which is one of the principal restraints of crime. There seems to be an assumption of guilt here. Nevertheless, he considers a false humanity seems opposed to this shortness of time. But all doubt, he believes, will vanish on reflection that the more defective any system of law is the greater are the dangers to which innocence is exposed.[1] The laws should fix a certain period of time both for the defence of the accused and for the discovery of proofs against him. But it would place the judge in the position of a legislator were it his duty to fix the time necessary for the latter.

Atrocious crimes, the memory of which stay long in the mind, deserve, when proved, no tradition in favour of the criminal. But lesser and obscure crimes should be allowed a certain assistance to help remove a man's uncertainty concerning his fate since the possibility of reform remains to him. Beccaria thinks it is sufficient to indicate these issues of principle because he is not able to fix a precise time limit except for a given system of laws in given social circumstances. He does, however, add that if the advantage of moderate penalties in a nation is proved, the laws which shorten or lengthen the term of prescription or of proofs, according to the seriousness of crimes, will supply an easy classification of a few mild punishments for a very large number of crimes.

But these periods of time will not be lengthened in exact proportion to the atrocity of crimes, since the probability of a crime is in inverse ratio to its violence. It will, then, be necessary to shorten the period for enquiry

---

1. We have already considered whether this view is mistaken in *Chapter 3*.

and increase that of prescription i.e. the time within which action may be taken and not be statute-barred. This might appear, he says, to contradict what he said before, namely, that it is possible to inflict equal penalties on unequal crimes by counting as a penalty that period of imprisonment which precedes the verdict. To explain this, he distinguishes two kinds of crimes – first, atrocious crimes beginning with homicide and including all excessive forms of wickedness, and, secondly, less serious crimes. The distinction, he claims, is founded on human nature.

Personal security is a natural right, the security of property a social one. The number of motives which impel men to violate their natural affections is far smaller than those which impel them, by their natural longing for happiness, to violate a right which they do not find written in their hearts but only in the conventions of society. The very great difference between the probability of these two kinds of crime respectively makes it necessary for them to be ruled by different principles. In cases of the more atrocious crimes, because they are more uncommon, the time for enquiry ought to be so much the less as the probability of the innocence of the accused is greater. And the time of prescription ought to be longer, as on an ultimate definite sentence of guilt or innocence depends the destruction of the hope of impunity, the harm of which is proportioned to the atrocity of the crime.

But in cases of lesser criminality, where the presumption in favour of a man's innocence is less, the time for enquiry should be longer and, as the harm of impunity (i.e. getting away with crime) is less, the time of prescription should be shorter. But such a division of crimes ought not be admitted if the danger of impunity decreases exactly in proportion to the greater probability of the crime. One should remember that an accused man, whose guilt or innocence is uncertain, may, though acquitted for lack of proofs, be arrested and subjected for the same crime to a fresh imprisonment and enquiry in the event of fresh legal proofs arising so long as the time of prescription allowed by the law has not been passed.[2]

There are some crimes which are at the same time of common occurrence and yet difficult to prove. In them the difficulty of proof is equivalent to a

---

2. In England a fresh trial was not possible under the rule of double jeopardy until this was modified and diluted by the Criminal Justice Act 2003.

probability of innocence. And the harm of their impunity being so much the less to be considered as their frequency depends on principles other than the risk of punishment. The time for enquiry and the period of prescription ought both to be proportionately less. Yet cases of adultery and homosexuality (see *Chapter 5*), both difficult to prove, are precisely those in which, according to received principles, tyrannical presumptions of *quasi-proofs* and *half-proofs* are allowed to prevail (as if a man could be *half-innocent* or *half-guilty*, in other words, *half-punishable* or *half-acquittable*). In these cases torture exercises its cruel sway over the person of the accused, over the witnesses, and even over the whole family of an unfortunate victim. And all this follows from the coldly wicked teaching of some doctors of law who set themselves up as the rule and standard for judges to follow.

In view of these principles it will appear strange (to anyone who does not reflect that reason has, so to speak, never yet legislated for a nation) that it is just the most atrocious crimes or that the most secret and insubstantial ones – that is those of least probability – which are proved by assumptions or by the weakest and most equivocal proofs. As if it were in the interests of the laws and the judges not to search for the truth but to find out the crime. As if the danger of condemning an innocent man were not so much the greater, the greater the probability of his innocence over that of his guilt.

The majority of mankind lack that vigour which is equally necessary for the greatest crimes as for the greatest virtues. Hence, it would appear that both extremes are contemporaneous phenomena in nations which depend rather on the energy of their government and of the passions that tend to the public good than on their size and the constant goodness of their laws. In the latter the weakened passions seem more adapted to maintain than to improve the form of government. From which flows an important consequence, namely, that great crimes in a nation do not always prove its decline.[3]

---

3. J.A. Farrer. (1880) *Crimes and Punishments including a new translation of Beccaria's Dei Delitti e Delle Pene.* London, Chatto & Windus, pp. 161-2.

Criminal Attempts

In general in present day English law a person is guilty of attempting to commit an offence if he does an act which is part of a series of acts which would constitute its actual commission if it were not interrupted. The mere intention to commit a criminal offence is not a crime, nor is an act merely preparatory to its commission. When Beccaria was writing the law was much the same in theory although the power to imprison without trial made a mockery of it. Nevertheless, he does say that the importance of preventing an attempt to commit a crime justifies a punishment for the attempt although it should be less than that for a crime actually committed. Particularly is this the case, he says, where there is an interval between the attempt and the execution of the crime and the thought of the greater punishment for the actual crime might lead to it not being carried out.

Accomplices

The same might be said, though for a different reason, where there are several accomplices to a crime, not all of them its actual perpetrators. In English law accomplices are liable to be tried and punished in the same manner as the principal offender. However, Beccaria believes that as with attempts they should not suffer so severe a punishment as the main perpetrator. When several men join together in an undertaking, he writes, the greater its risk is, the more they will seek to make the threat of punishment equal for all of them. The more difficult it will be, therefore, to find one of them who will be willing to actually execute the crime if in doing so he thereby incurs a greater chance of a more severe punishment than his fellows. In that sense it can be seen as a deterrent. The only exception to this would be where the perpetrator receives a larger part of the proceeds of the crime as compensation for his undertaking a greater risk.

Some courts, says Beccaria, offer a pardon to an accomplice in a serious crime if he is willing to betray his companions. This is an expedient which has drawbacks as well as advantages. The advantages of the practice are that it helps prevent crimes and the intimidation of the people because the results are visible whilst the authors remain hidden. Moreover, it also helps to show that a man who violates the public law is likely also to break private contracts.

On the other hand, one disadvantage is that in offering such a pardon the law authorises treachery, which is detested even by criminals. It introduces crimes of cowardice which are far more pernicious to a nation than crimes of courage. Courage is not common, but it only wants a benevolent power to direct it to actions that benefit the public good. Cowardice, by contrast, is more common and is a self-interested and contagious evil which can never be turned into a virtue. Besides, a tribunal which calls in aid the law-breaker proclaims its own uncertainty and the weakness of the laws themselves by taking the assistance of those who have violated them.

Beccaria believes, however, that a general law promising a reward to an accomplice who exposes a crime would be preferable to a special declaration in every particular case, because in this way the mutual fear which each accomplice would have of his own risk would tend to prevent their association. The court would not make criminals audacious by showing that their aid is called for in a particular case. Such a law, however, should accompany the pardon with transportation.

But it is in vain, he adds, that the criminal should torment himself in order to extinguish the remorse he feels in attempting to authorise the inviolable laws, the monument of public confidence and basis of human morality, to resort to treachery and lying. What an example to the nation it would be where the promised pardon is not observed and where the man who had responded to it is dragged by legal quibbles to punishment in spite of the promise. Such examples are not rare in some countries. That is why political society is regarded as a complex machine, the springs of which are moved by the strongest and most powerful people.

Evidence and Proofs of a Crime

According to Beccaria, the following general formulae are very helpful in determining the certainty of a fact.

When the proofs of a crime are dependent on each other, that is, when the evidence of each witness, taken separately, proves nothing; or when all the proofs are dependent on one, the number of proofs do not increase or diminish the probability of the fact for the force of the whole is no greater than the force of that on which they depend. If this fails they all fall to the ground. When the proofs are independent of each other the probability of the fact increases in proportion to the number of proofs since the falsehood of one does not diminish the veracity of another.

It may seem extraordinary, says Beccaria, to speak of probability with regard to crimes which, to merit a punishment, must be proved. But this paradox vanishes when it is considered that, strictly speaking, moral certainty is only probability. It is called a certainty because every man in his senses assents to it from a habit produced by the necessity of acting. That certainty which is necessary to decide that the accused is guilty is the very same which guides every man in the most important transactions in his life.

The proofs of a crime may be divided into two classes, perfect and imperfect. Beccaria calls those perfect which exclude the possibility of innocence and imperfect those which do not do so. Of the first, one proof alone is sufficient for condemnation. Of the second, as many are necessary as are required to make a single perfect proof. That is to say that, though each of these, taken separately, does not exclude the possibility of innocence, it is nevertheless excluded when they are taken together.

It should also be noted that the imperfect proofs from which an accused person, if innocent, has it in his power to clear himself but declines to do so, become perfect. This moral certainty of proofs, however, is easier to feel than to define exactly. For this reason the best law is one which provides assistants, taken by lot not by selection, to aid the principal judge. For that ignorance which decides by sentiment is less likely to be wrong than the knowledge of the laws which judge by opinion. Where the laws are clear and precise the function of a judge is merely to ascertain the facts.

If for searching out the proofs of a crime ability and cleverness are required, and if in the presentation of the result clearness and precision are essential, all that is required to judge of the result itself is simple and common good sense. This is a faculty which is less illogical than the learning of a judge accustomed to finding men guilty and reducing everything to an artificial system borrowed from his studies. Happy is the nation where laws are not a science! This last is a curious proposition coming from Beccaria and contradicts what he says elsewhere. But it was left to Bentham to make strenuous efforts with his numerous legal codes to make the law more scientific and determinist.

Nevertheless, going back to his principles Beccaria says it is an admirable law which provides that everyone shall be tried by his peers for when life, liberty and fortune are at stake those sentiments which inequality inspires should have no voice. The feeling of superiority with which the fortunate look upon the unfortunate, and that envy with which an inferior regards his superior should have no influence. But when the crime in question is an offence against a person of a different rank from the accused then half the jury should be peers of the accused and the other half peers of the person offended. In this way only will the voice of the laws and the truth be heard. Whatever the merits of this proposal were in Beccaria's day it is inappropriate now when, in England at least, all members of the jury are randomly selected and, to a certain degree, can be challenged by either side in the trial.

It is also just, says Beccaria, that the accused should have the liberty, up to a certain point, of refusing jurors whom he may suspect of bias or prejudice against him. If he is allowed to do so for some time without opposition he will appear to condemn himself. As they often were not on the continent, both trials and verdicts should be public in open court as it is the cement of society that people may say "We are protected by the laws". Furthermore, an accused person should be allowed to give evidence which was an important principle not operating at the time on the European continent or in England.

Witnesses

It is vital, stresses Beccaria, to determine exactly the credibility of witnesses and the proofs of guilt. Every person of common sense may be a witness. But the credibility of their evidence is measured by the interest they have in speaking or concealing the truth. Hence, nothing can be more frivolous than to reject the evidence of women on the pretext of their feebleness, or more childish than not to admit the evidence of those who are under sentence of death because they are said to be "dead in law". In support of this silly metaphor many victims have been sacrificed. Provided that the testimony of a condemned criminal does not stop the course of justice why, in the interests of truth, should he not be allowed to adduce new evidence? And how irrational to exclude persons branded with ill-repute. In all these cases such witnesses should be listened to when they have no interest in lying. The credibility of a witness then should only diminish in proportion to the hatred, friendship or connections subsisting between him and the accused.

More than one witness is necessary to establish a crime because when the accused denies what the witness affirms nothing is proved and the right that everyone has to be believed innocent prevails. The credibility of a witness is reduced the greater the improbability of the crime such as witchcraft or acts of wanton cruelty. Some writers on penal law have adopted a contrary view, namely that the credibility of a witness is greater if the crime is more atrocious. They say that in the most vicious crimes (i.e. the least probable) the slightest conjectures are sufficient and the judge is to be allowed to exceed the limits of the law. This is an inhuman attitude dictated by cruel stupidity. Judges and lawyers whose opinions, when alive, were biased and unjust but which after their death became decisive authority in the name of precedent, are the arbiters of the lives and fortunes of the people. They are alarmed at the thought of condemning some innocent person and, as a consequence, they have burdened the law with superfluous formalities and exceptions, the exact observance of which would cause anarchy to sit on the throne of justice.

Finally, the evidence of a witness is almost null and void when the spoken words of another are construed as a crime. After all, the tone, the gesture, all that precedes or follows the different ideas attached by people to the same words, so alter and modify a person's utterances that it is almost impossible to repeat them exactly as they were spoken. Moreover, actions of a violent and unusual character, such as real crimes are, leave their traces in numberless circumstances and effects that flow from them. Words only remain in the memory of their hearers and memory is for the most part unfaithful and often deceitful. It is on this account so much easier to fix a false charge upon a person's words than upon their actions.

William Garrow[4]

There is no evidence to show that William Garrow had any knowledge of Beccaria's book. But it was available in translation in England and it would be pleasing to think that it helped to inspire his fight for justice. On the other hand, living in Italy before Garrow appeared at the Old Bailey in London, Beccaria would not have been aware of the advent of adversary trial in England. But what he said as described in the preceding paragraphs shows precisely why adversary trial and cross-examination of witnesses is so significant.

Prior to Garrow, in the late eighteenth century a prisoner could not have counsel to represent him in court whilst the prosecutor could. The ancient reason for this injustice was that prosecutions were taken in the name of the sovereign and it was considered *lese majesty* to have the Crown challenged by a lawyer. As a consequence, prisoners were often led into court completely bemused and overawed by their surroundings for a short trial in which they often said nothing or very little. Sometimes they were even returned to their cells completely unaware that they had been found guilty and faced the death penalty or transportation. Equally, there was no presumption of innocence or rules of evidence to assist prisoners.

In eighteenth century England thief-takers were paid by the government a small fortune in blood money for obtaining a conviction against a criminal. But how was it decided if a person was a criminal? Very often it was solely on the evidence of those very thief-takers. Perjury was rife and an untold number of victims were sent to the gallows or transportation solely on the basis of fabricated evidence and downright lies. This is where the importance of William Garrow and other barristers at the Old Bailey lies in exposing the thief-takers to juries and securing the establishment of adversariality and rules of criminal evidence that assisted prisoners in court by giving them previously unknown rights. It cannot be doubted that Beccaria would have applauded heartily.

---

4. For more on Garrow and his impact on adversary trial, see John Hostettler and Richard Braby. (2009) *Sir William Garrow: His Life, Times and Fight for Justice*. Hampshire, Waterside Press.

Imprisonment

In the eighteenth century conditions in Europe's prisons were indescribably appalling as Beccaria would have known at first hand from his friend Alessandro Verri. Ill-treatment, extortion and debauchery were commonplace. Since hanging is relatively mild compared with being beaten, burned or lashed to death in an agonizing manner so, Beccaria thinks, it can be less terrible than imprisonment. Particularly in France where *lettres de cachet* were widely used by powerful and religious zealots to secure the imprisonment of their perceived enemies in dark and dank dungeons like the Bastille without trial.

These *lettres* were discretionary, arbitrary and often secret orders issued by the King of France to secure certain acts including imprisonment. They were handed out indiscriminately to courtiers and sometimes even signed and given out blank. They were abolished by the Constituent Assembly in the French Revolution and briefly restored by Napoleon.

To Beccaria this is infamous. He declares, "That a magistrate, the executor of the laws, should have a power to imprison a citizen, to deprive the man he hates of his liberty upon frivolous pretences, and to leave his friend unpunished, notwithstanding the strongest proofs of his guilt, is an error, as common, as it is contrary to the aim of society, which is personal security."[5]

As he says, in his day imprisonment is a punishment that differs from all others in Europe in that it precedes conviction. Naturally, he considers that like other punishments it should only be inflicted when decreed by law which should determine the crime and what evidence is necessary to justify the detention of the accused, his questioning and punishment. In other words, he might be held on remand. Imprisonment might also be justified if the defendant freely confesses, runs away, or continues to menace the person injured – but based on the law and not the whim of the judges whose decisions when they do not follow the law are against political liberty.

Beccaria is adamant that a person accused, imprisoned, tried and acquitted should not be branded with disgrace. This was not always what happened because the existing system of penal laws was based on power rather than

---

5. J.A. Farrer. (1880) *Crimes and Punishments including a New Translation of Beccaria's Dei Delitti e Delle Pene*. London, Chatto & Windus, p. 132.

justice. The accused and the convicted were thrown indiscriminately into the same prison and imprisonment was regarded as a punishment and a stigma rather than a means of holding a person pending trial. If an innocent person were released the stain of his incarceration stuck to him and many people believed that there was "no smoke without fire".

John Howard

It was his imprisonment in the dungeon of a French prison that led John Howard, England's pioneering prison reformer, to inspect prison conditions in his own country in the 1770s. His published conclusions revealed that often prisoners were so starved that they could hardly move, that many slept on rags or on the floor and many, including women, were kept at all times in irons, even at night when asleep. However, Howard's desire to reform prison conditions was tempered by his wish to reform prisoners by harsh discipline. Hence, alongside improving conditions in prisons he saw virtue in prisoners spending long periods in solitary confinement to reflect on their sins and achieve reformation.

Even his desire to alleviate conditions was slow in coming since although some of his proposals were incorporated into statutes they were not mandatory and the prison authorities and supervising justices largely ignored them. Unlike Beccaria's work, Howard's book received no instant recognition or acclamation that led to action. It was not until Sir Robert Peel became Home Secretary in 1822 that real change commenced based upon Howard's published exposures. Nevertheless, when Howard died of typhus on 20 January 1790, in a military hospital in the Ukraine after inspecting conditions there, Bentham said of him, "he died a martyr after living an apostle".

Voltaire

In his Commentary on Beccaria's book Voltaire wrote that whereas after he is hanged a man is good for nothing, punishments invented for the good of society ought to be useful to society. It is evident, he said, that a score of stout robbers, condemned for life to some public work, would serve the state and the community whilst hanging them would benefit nobody but the executioner. Thieves in England, he said, somewhat overstating the position, were seldom punished with death but were transported to the colonies. This was also practised in Russia and not one criminal was executed during the reign of the autocratic empress Elizabeth. Yet crimes were not multiplied by this humanity. On the contrary, the exiles continued to labour for a living and they married and multiplied.

CHAPTER 7

OTHER PUNISHMENTS

Crimes of Violence

After the crime of high treason, writes Beccaria, in terms of seriousness come crimes of violence against individuals and their liberty. Since the personal security of individuals is the primary aim of society the breach of such security merits one of the severest punishments that the law allows. Not all crimes affect the person, however, as some are committed against property. The first should be dealt with by corporal punishment. They include murder and theft and crimes committed by the powerful.

The rich should not have it in their power to atone for a crime against the weak and the poor by a cash payment. For then wealth, which under the protection of the law should be the reward of industry, would encourage tyranny. And, then you will see the powerful employ their advantage to select from the accumulation of civil relations those which most favour their interests. This is the magic art that transforms citizens into beasts of burden and which, in the hands of the strong, is the chain that binds the weak and unwise. Liberty is at an end when, in certain cases, the law permits a man to cease to be a person and become an object. Thus it is that in some governments, where there is all the appearance of liberty, tyranny lies concealed and insinuates itself into some neglected corner of the constitution where it gathers strength unseen. Men generally resolutely oppose the assaults of barefaced and open tyranny but disregard the little insect that gnaws through the dike and opens a sure though secret passage to flooding.

Punishment of Nobles

Beccaria pays special attention to the punishment of nobles whose privileges he believes make up a great part of the laws of many different countries.

He does not wish to consider whether the hereditary distinction between aristocrats and commoners is useful to a government or whether it forms an intermediate power useful in moderating the excesses of both extremes. Nor whether, supposing it to be true that inequality is inevitable and useful in society, it be also true that such inequality should subsist between classes rather than individuals. Instead, he confines himself to the punishments suitable for nobles and he asserts that the punishment of a nobleman should in no way differ from that of the lowest member of society.

It is possible that the wisest and most industrious citizens should obtain the greatest honours but they should not, therefore, fear less than others violating those conditions on which they are raised above others. It may be objected, he continues, that the same punishments inflicted upon a nobleman and a commoner are in reality different because of the difference in their education and the humiliation it reflects upon a renowned family. But, as indicated earlier he considers that punishments are to be estimated, not by the feelings of the criminal, but by the injury done to society by a person's crime, which injury is made worse by the high station of the offender.

Nonetheless, Beccaria favoured the aristocracy and bourgeois and mercantile elements in their struggle against monarchy in Europe although his book severely undermined the power of both. In favouring the aristocracy he took a similar attitude to what happened in England in 1688 with the Glorious Revolution. Although there were some differences in what Beccaria favoured and that revolution, the effect of both was to undermine absolute monarchy and ultimately the nobility. The events in England signalled the partial triumph of the propertied Whigs over royal despotism and at last the common law was to be supreme over the royal prerogative and the rule of law began to displace royal discrimination. But in much of Europe monarchy, for a time, survived the civilizing changes wrought in the penal laws that existed for the protection of monarchs and rulers generally.

Theft and Robbery

For Beccaria theft without violence should be punished by fines on the principle that he who tries to enrich himself with the property of another should be deprived of part of his own. However, this crime often results from the misery and despair that comes from endeavouring to survive on a bare existence. Moreover, monetary punishments may increase the number of robbers by increasing the number of poor, and may deprive an innocent family of subsistence. The most fitting punishment is to pass the benefit of the labour of the criminal to society until he has made restitution for his theft and violation of the social contract. This is similar, of course, to the modern theory and practice of service to the community.

Robbery with violence, on the other hand, should additionally result in corporal punishment as well as imprisonment. But the punishment should not include flogging or the pillory. Other writers, he says, have shown the abuse that arises from a failure to distinguish between the punishment appropriate for robbery with violence and theft by fraud. They make a sum of money equivalent to a man's life. For these crimes are of a different nature and in politics, as in mathematics, qualities of different natures are entirely separate. Political machinery more than anything else retains the motion originally given to it, and is the slowest to adapt itself to a fresh one.

Voltaire, for his part, considered that in countries where a trifling domestic theft or breach of trust was punished with death, the punishment was disproportionate and dangerous to society. It was even an encouragement to larceny. If a master prosecuted his servant and the unhappy man suffered death the whole neighbourhood held the matter in abhorrence. They perceived that the law was contrary to nature and consequently that it was a bad law. The result was that masters, to avoid blame, contented themselves with discharging the thief who afterwards stole from another and gradually became more dishonest. The punishment being the same for a small theft as for a greater he would naturally steal as much as he could and at last would not scruple to turn assassin to prevent detection.

If, on the contrary, the punishment was proportioned to the crime and those who were guilty of a breach of trust were condemned to labour for the public, the master would not hesitate to bring the offender to justice and the crime would be less frequently committed. It was also true that rigorous laws often produced crimes.

Ill-repute

Injuries which affect honour, that is the proper esteem every citizen has a right to expect from others, should be punished with public dishonour. Disgrace is a mark of public disapproval which deprives the culprit of the goodwill and confidence of his fellow citizens and the fraternity existing between members of the same society. This cannot always be dealt with by the law. It is therefore necessary that the disgrace inflicted by law should be the same as that which results from the nature of things, from universal morality or the particular system adopted by nations. If, on the contrary, law and morality differ from one another either the law will no longer be respected or ideas of morality and virtue will vanish in spite of the preaching of moralists which are always too weak to resist the force of example. If we declare actions infamous that are in reality merely indifferent, we lessen the infamy of those that are really disgraceful.

Public disgrace should not be used as a punishment too frequently since the power of opinion grows weaker by repetition. Nor should it be inflicted upon a number of persons at the same time for the disgrace of many resolves itself into the infamy of one. Painful and corporal punishments should never be applied to fanaticism since being based on pride it glories in persecution. Only public disgrace and ridicule should be employed against fanatics so that public pride overrules the vanity of the fanatic. In this way, by opposing one passion to another and opinion to opinion, an end is put to the admiration of the public caused by a false principle the original absurdity of which is concealed. This is the way to avoid bedevilling the invariable nature of things which, operating incessantly, overturn and destroy regulations which contradict the law. It is not only in the fine arts that the imitation of nature is a fundamental principle. It is the same in sound policy which is the art of uniting and directing to the same end the natural and immutable feelings of mankind.

Rewards for Detaining or Killing Criminals

Is it advantageous to society, asks Beccaria, to set a reward on the head of a criminal and to make every citizen an executioner by arming him against the offender? If the offender has taken refuge in another country, by offering a reward the sovereign encourages his subjects themselves to commit a crime and expose themselves to punishment and is thereby guilty of taking on the authority of another state and encouraging others to do the same. If, however, the criminal still remains in his own country, to set a price upon his head is strong proof of the weakness of the government. If he has the strength to defend himself he will not seek the assistance of another.

Moreover, such an edict overturns all ideas of morality and virtue which are always ready to vanish from the human mind at the slightest breath. With one hand the laws punish treachery, whilst with the other they encourage it. With one hand the lawgiver strengthens ties of kindred and friendship and with the other rewards the violation of both. In contradiction with himself, at one time he invites the suspicious minds of men to mutual confidence and at another he plants distrust in every heart. Instead of preventing one crime he causes a hundred. Such are the expedients of weak nations whose laws are like temporary repairs to a ruined, tottering building.

On the contrary, as a nation becomes enlightened good faith and mutual confidence become necessary. Then tricks, intrigues and obscure and indirect actions are more easily discovered and the interest of the community is better secured against the passions of the individual. Even past times of ignorance, when private virtue was encouraged by public morality, provide examples to more enlightened times. But laws which reward treachery and stir up hidden passions by spreading suspicion among citizens excite stealthy wars and mutual distrust and oppose the necessary union of morality and jurisprudential principles and policy which is the foundation of happiness and universal peace.

Certainly in England in the eighteenth century, when there was no adequate police force, government did not hesitate to offer rewards, which became known as "blood money", to those who gave evidence against often innocent people who were tried and convicted. As we have seen in *Chapter 6*, this led to a number of men, called "thief takers", committing perjury which resulted in many miscarriages of justice and transportation or death for their victims. It was this practice that barrister William Garrow destroyed with savage wit and bitter cross-examination of such "witnesses".[1] His courage against a large body of hostile lawyers who considered themselves his superiors encouraged other Old Bailey barristers to adopt similar tactics. As a consequence, there was gradually built up a body of rules of evidence to assist defendants, as well as the presumption of innocence and eventually the right of a defendant to be represented in full by counsel after the enactment of the Prisoners' Counsel Act 1836. English criminal procedure was transformed and the new system spread to all common law countries and today many other jurisdictions across the globe are adopting it.

Criminal Procedure

This meant that in the eighteenth century adversary trial, with its battle between barristers on both sides in a criminal trial, was emerging in England where it had a revolutionary impact upon criminal procedure. It was soon to spread to many parts of the world with beneficial effects upon rules of evidence and human rights. However, its significance was to go unrecognised by judges, lawyers, jurists and researchers until relatively modern times when conflict has become a key social issue.[2] Great jurists such as Blackstone, Holdsworth, Fitzjames Stephen and others including members of the Bar, all failed to see the rise of adversary trial and the role of Garrow in these events, possibly because their eyes did not fall upon the "obnoxious" Old Bailey and its barristers who were regarded as beyond the pale. As Allyson N. May has shown these barristers were widely regarded, inside and outside the profession, as "Old Bailey hacks" and dishonest ruffians exercising low standards of advocacy.[3]

What Stephen, who was a barrister and a judge, actually wrote was:

---

1. See John Hostettler. (2006) *Fighting for Justice: The History and Origins of Adversary Trial.* Hook, Waterside Press.
2. *Ibid.*
3. Allyson, N. May. (2003) *The Bar and the Old Bailey, 1750-1850.* Chapel Hill and London, The University of North Carolina Press.

> The *most remarkable change* into the practice of the courts [in the eighteenth century] was the process by which the old rule which deprived prisoners of the assistance of counsel in trials for felony was gradually relaxed. A practice sprung up, *the growth of which cannot now be traced,* by which counsel were allowed to do everything for prisoners accused of felony except addressing the jury for them.[4] (italics added)

In addition to his forceful and ironic cross-examinations of "thief-takers", Garrow was a pioneer in using the cross-examination as a means to comment on the evidence to the jury and aggressively put up a fight for the accused. But since neither Stephen nor anyone else, until the last few decades, could trace the origins of adversary trial it is not surprising that Voltaire has nothing to say on the question although in his Commentary on Beccaria's book he did write on criminal procedure. (Beccaria, on the other hand, wrote his book before Garrow exploded on to the scene at the Old Bailey).

Voltaire

Our criminal procedure, Voltaire wrote, appeared in many instances to point only at the destruction of the accused. It was the only law that was uniform throughout the whole kingdom; a law which should certainly be no less favourable to the innocent than terrible to the accused. In England, he wrote, a man might recover damages for false imprisonment. In France, on the contrary, an innocent person who had the misfortune to be thrown into a dungeon and tortured almost to death had no damages to hope for, no action against anyone. And, to add to his misfortune his joints had been dislocated and he had forever lost his reputation. It was said that severity was required for the discovery of crimes as in a war of human justice against iniquity. But there was generosity and compassion even in war and anyway should the law delight in barbarity?

In ancient Rome, said Voltaire, evidence was heard in public in the presence of the accused who might answer or interrogate witnesses and employ counsel. The procedure was open and noble; it breathed Roman magnanimity.

---

4. James Fitzjames Stephen. (1883) *A History of the Criminal Law of England.* London, Macmillan, vol. i, p. 424.

In France, a trial was conducted in secret. A single judge, attended only by his clerk, heard each witness separately. The law seemed to oblige the magistrate to be the enemy of the accused rather than his judge. It was left to the decision of the magistrate whether to confront the witnesses with the accused as he thought fit. "Amazing! That so necessary a part of the procedure should be left indeterminate". He concluded that in his age governments claimed universally to be aiming at perfection. They should not therefore neglect to perfect the laws upon which lives and fortunes depended.[5]

Mildness of Punishments

At the very core of Beccaria's philosophy is the concept that wherever possible punishment should be lenient. Cruelty is useless and an instrument either of furious fanatics or weak tyrants. He frequently contends that it is evident that the purpose of punishments should neither be to torment human beings nor to undo a crime already committed. The shrieks of an unhappy prisoner cannot call back from ever-receding time actions already carried out. He is convinced that crimes are more effectually prevented by the certainty rather than the severity of punishment. This calls for vigilance by the magistrates and severity in a judge. If it is to be a useful virtue, it has to be tempered by lenient laws. The object of punishment is simply to prevent the criminal from again injuring his fellow citizens and to deter others from committing similar injuries. Those punishments and the method of inflicting them should be preferred which, duly proportioned to the offence, will produce a more efficient and lasting impression on the minds of men and inflict the least torture on the body of a criminal.

Who can read history, he asks, without being horror-struck at the barbarous and useless torments which men who were called wise devised and executed in cold blood? Who is there but must feel his blood boil when he regards the thousands of sufferers whom misery, either intended or tolerated by the laws which have always favoured the few and outraged the many,

---

5. Cesare Beccaria. (1775) *An Essay on Crimes and Punishments with a Commentary by Monsieur Voltaire.* London, F. Newbery, p. lxxv.

has driven to a desperate return to the original state of nature - or of those accused of impossible crimes or of being guilty only of having been true to their own principles? Who could, without horror, think of their being torn to pieces with slow and deliberate barbarity by men endowed with the same feelings?

The certainty of a small punishment would make a stronger impression than the fear of a more severe one accompanied with hopes of escaping punishment altogether. After all, it is in the nature of man to be terrified at the approach of the smallest inevitable evil, whilst hope has the power of dispelling fear of a greater harm. The success of a first crime has often driven men to further crimes and if punishments be very severe men naturally tend to commit other crimes to avoid being punished for the first crime. The countries and times in which punishments have been fiercest were always those in which the most bloody and inhuman actions were committed since the lawmaker and the assassin were imbued with the same spirit of cruelty.

In proportion as punishments become more cruel, the minds of men, like a fluid rising to the same height with that which surrounds it, grow hardened and insensible. From the power of emotions, in the space of a hundred years the wheel ceases to terrify any more than a prison. For a punishment to produce the effect required it is sufficient that the evil it occasions should exceed the advantage expected from the crime, taking into account the certainty of the punishment and the loss of the advantage. All severity beyond this is superfluous and therefore tyrannical.

Men regulate their conduct by the repeated impression of evils they know and not by reason of evils they ignore. Beccaria points to two examples. First, he says, consider two nations. In one the most severe punishment is indefinite slavery, and in the other it is breaking on the wheel. Both would induce the same degree of terror. There can be no reason for increasing the punishments of the first which are not equally valid for augmenting those of the second to more lasting and more ingenious modes of tormenting, and so on to the most exquisite refinements of a science too well-known to tyrants.

There are two other consequences of cruel punishments which counteract their intention to prevent crime. The first arises from the impossibility of establishing an exact proportion between the crime and the punishment. Though ingenious cruelty has greatly multiplied the variety of torments yet the human frame can suffer only to a given degree beyond which it is impossible to proceed however serious the crime. The second consequence is the opportunity of being allowed to get away with the crime. Human nature is limited no less in evil than in good. Excessive barbarity can never be more than temporary; it is impossible that is should be supported by a permanent system of legislation. For if the laws are too cruel they will have to be changed or anarchy and impunity will follow.

The Means of Preventing Crimes

Beccaria devotes a section of his book to how to prevent crimes since it is better, he writes, to prevent crimes than to punish them. This is the chief aim of every system of good legislation, which is the art of guiding men to the greatest possible happiness and the least possible misery. But previously the means employed for this purpose had been generally inadequate and contrary to the end required. It is impossible to reduce the tumultuous activity of men and women to absolute regularity and human laws cannot entirely prevent disorders in society. Such, however, is the belief of weak men when invested with authority. To prohibit a number of trivial activities does not result in the prevention of crimes they may produce but often creates new ones.

It redefines virtue and vice which at other times are held to be eternal and immutable. We should be reduced to a terrible situation if everything were to be forbidden that might possibly lead to a crime. It would deprive men of the use of their senses. For one motive that drives a man to commit a real crime there are a thousand which excite him to commit those trivial activities which are called crimes by bad laws. If then the probability that a crime will be committed is in proportion to the number of motives, to extend the sphere of crimes would be to increase that probability. The majority of the laws are nothing but privileges or a tribute paid by all to the advantage of a few.

If we wish to prevent crimes let the laws be clear and simple. Let the entire nation be united in their protection. Let them be aimed to favour all instead of particular classes of people. Let the laws be feared and only the laws. Fear of the law is salutary whilst the fear of men is a fruitful and fatal source of crimes. Men who are enslaved are more immoral and cruel than those who are free. The latter study the sciences and the interests of their country. They aspire to great things and imitate them. But those whose views are confined to the immediate find themselves distracted by depravity.

If you desire to prevent crimes, declares Beccaria, then ensure the laws are clear and simple, that the whole force of the nation is brought to bear to defend them and that no part of them is destroyed. Make the law favour men as individuals and not classes of men. Fear of the law can be beneficial but the fear of one man of another is fatal and can cause crime. If uncertainty of the laws affects a nation its ignorance is maintained and increased. If it affects a nation, which though fond of pleasure is also full of energy, it wastes that energy in a number of petty intrigues which spread distrust and make treachery and lying the foundation of prudence. On the other hand, if it affects a courageous and brave nation, the uncertainty is ultimately destroyed after many swings from liberty to slavery and from slavery back again to liberty.

Science

To prevent crimes it is necessary to ensure that liberty is tempered with enlightenment. The evils that flow from knowledge are in inverse ratio to its dissemination; the benefits directly proportioned to it. A bold imposter, who is never a commonplace man, is adored by an ignorant people, despised by an enlightened one. Knowledge makes the comparison of objects easier by showing them in different aspects. When the clouds of ignorance are dispelled by the glow of knowledge, authority trembles, but the force of the laws remains immovable. Knowledge, by facilitating comparisons between objects and multiplying men's points of view, brings many different notions into comparison, causing them to modify one another, all the more easily as the same views and the same difficulties are observed in others.

In a reference again to the social contract theory, Beccaria asserts that whilst the power of the law remains unshaken no educated person has any dislike of the clear public contracts which secure the common safety. When he compares the trifling and useless liberty he has sacrificed with the sum total of all the liberties sacrificed by others who without the laws might have been hostile to him. When a sensitive person contemplates a code of well-made laws and finds that he has only lost the liberty of injuring others he will feel nothing but satisfaction.

It is false to believe that the sciences have always been prejudicial to mankind. When they were so, evil was inevitable. The multiplication of the human species on the face of the earth introduced war and the rudiments of arts and the first laws perished. This was the first philosophy of man and its few aspects were just because his lack of wisdom preserved him from error. But with necessities increasing with the number of mankind, stronger and more lasting impressions were required to prevent their frequent relapse into a state of barbarity.

The first religious errors which peopled the earth with false divinities, and created a world of invisible beings to govern the visible creation, were of the utmost service to mankind. The greatest benefactors to humanity were those who dared to deceive and lead ignorance to the foot of the altar. By presenting to the minds of the ignorant things beyond their senses they united men's emotions towards a single object which absorbed them. This was the age which embodied the first transition of all nations from a state of savagery. As it is in the nature of error to sub-divide itself *ad infinitum,* so the pretended knowledge that sprang from it transformed mankind into a blind multitude destroying each other in the labyrinth in which they were enclosed. Hence it follows that some sensible and philosophical minds went so far as to regret the ancient state of barbarity. This was the first epoch in which knowledge, or rather opinions, were harmful.

The second age was found in the difficult passage from error to truth, from darkness to enlightenment. The violent shock between a mass of errors, useful to the few and powerful, and the truths so important to the many and the weak, with the fermentation of emotions produced infinite evils to unfortunate men. In the study of history, periods, after certain intervals, resemble each other. And we frequently find, in the necessary passage from the obscurity of ignorance to the light of philosophy, and from tyranny to liberty, one generation is sacrificed to the next. But when this flame is extinguished, and the world delivered from its evils, truth, after very slow progress, is worshipped in the assemblies of nations. It is impossible to believe that light diffused among the people is more destructive than darkness and that knowledge about the relations of things can ever be harmful to mankind.

Ignorance may be less harmful than a small degree of knowledge, because the latter adds to the harm of ignorance the inevitable errors of a narrow view of things. But a man of enlightened understanding, appointed guardian of the law, is the greatest blessing that can be bestowed on a nation. Such a man is used to facing the truth and not fearing it. He considers the nation as his family and his fellow-citizens as brothers. A philosopher has interests unknown to ordinary people. He should not deny in public principles that he preaches in private or the habit of loving truth for its own sake. A few such philosophers can mould the happiness of a nation which, however, would be of short duration if good laws did not increase their number and diminish the likelihood of improper choices.[6]

Magistrates

Bearing in mind the nature of the courts at the time, Beccaria also believes that another way of preventing crimes is to interest the magistrates who carry out the laws in seeking to preserve rather than corrupt them. And the greater the number of men who compose the magistracy the less danger there will be of their exercising any undue power over the law. For corruption is more difficult among men who are under the close observation of one another, and their inducement to increase their individual authority diminishes in proportion to the smallness of the share of it that can fall to each of them.

On the other hand, if the legislature, by the pomp, formality and severity of laws, and by refusal to hear the grievances, whether true or false, of the man who thinks himself oppressed, accustoms people to fear the magistrates more than the laws, the magistrates will benefit but at the cost of private and public security.

---

6. Cesare Beccaria. *An Essay on Crimes and Punishments with a Commentary by Monsieur de Voltaire. Op. cit.* pp. 167-172.

Certainty of Punishments–Pardons

As we have seen, Beccaria considers that one of the best means of preventing crimes is not the cruelty of the punishments for committing them but the certainty of punishment under a mild system of laws. The inevitability of punishment, even though moderate, makes a stronger impression than the fear of a more terrible one but which is associated with the hope of impunity. Even the least evils, when certain, always terrify men's minds whilst hope throws into the distance the idea of greater evils, especially when buoyed up by the impunity which greed and weakness encourage.

Curiously, Beccaria is opposed to a victim pardoning an offender who is guilty of a minor crime. Such an act is merciful and human, he says, but contrary to public policy as if a private citizen could do away with the necessity of example. The right to punish does not rest with an individual but with the community as a whole.

If punishments become milder, as Beccaria proposes, he believes that clemency and pardon by the executive, once sentence had been pronounced by a court, will also become less necessary. Happy, therefore, will be the nation in which clemency and pardon will be considered as dangerous. Clemency should be excluded in legislation where punishments are mild and criminal procedure regular and speedy. This might seem cruel to those living in the chronic state of the criminal law where absurd laws and the severity of punishments make pardons and clemency necessary. But clemency is a virtue vested in the legislature and not the courts and it should shine in the legal code and not in private judgment.

To show criminals that crimes are sometimes pardoned, and that punishment does not always follow, is to nourish the flattering hope of impunity and cause them to consider every punishment inflicted as an act of injustice and oppression. In pardoning, the sovereign surrenders public security in favour of an individual and proclaims a public act of escape. The judges should be severe but the legislature mild, merciful and humane. Let it found its laws on the basis of self-love and the general interest. Then it will no longer be constrained by partial laws and violent remedies to separate at every moment the public welfare from that of individuals and to raise the appearance of public security on fear and mistrust.

False Ideas of Utility

Injustice can be caused by legislators entertaining false ideas about utility. For example, to think more of the inconvenience to individuals than the community. It is a false idea of utility to sacrifice a thousand real advantages for one trifling drawback, which would deprive men of the use of fire because it burns or of water because it drowns, and subject the innocent to vexations which only the guilty deserve. It is a false idea of utility which, sacrificing the thing to the name, distinguishes the public good from that of every individual member of the public. There is this difference between the state of society and the state of nature, that in the latter a savage only commits injuries against others with a view to benefitting himself; whilst in the former state men are sometimes moved by bad laws to injure others without any corresponding benefit to themselves. The tyrant casts fear and dread into the minds of others, but they return to torment his own breast.[7]

Family Spirit

Fatal and legalised injustices have been approved by the wisest of men and practised by the most free republics owing to their having regarded society as an aggregate of families rather than as one of individuals. Here, perhaps based upon his own experience with his father, Beccaria is considering the family as a form of slavery. Suppose, he says, there are 100,000 individuals, or 20,000 families of five persons each including the head of the family. If the association is constituted by families it will consist of 20,000 men and 80,000 subordinates. If it is an association of individuals it will consist of 100,000 citizens and not a single subordinate person.

In the first case a monarchical spirit will arise but in the second case the republican spirit will breathe, not only in the market places and meetings of the people but also within the home where lies so great a part of human happiness or misery. Family spirit is a spirit of detail whereas community

---

7. J. A. Farrer.(1880) *Crimes and Punishments including a new translation of Beccaria's Dei Delitti e Delle Pene.* London, Chatto & Windus, pp. 233-5.

spirit seeks the welfare of the greater number. But Beccaria fails to appreciate that families are often a greater factor in ensuring success to communities than individuals.

Even so, Beccaria accepts that there will be subordination in both a community of individuals and a community of families but sees the subordination as voluntary in the first case and secured by compulsion in the second. He considers that private morality inspires fear and subjection whilst public morality teaches courage and freedom. One calls for constant sacrifice of oneself to a vain idol called "the good of the family", the other teaches men to benefit themselves and sacrifice themselves to the good of their country. It is difficult to understand Beccaria's reasoning in this instance although we must consider it was born in the cauldron of the lives of poverty and despair in which a large proportion of Italian people lived during his day.

Voltaire's Commentary[8]

In his Commentary on *Crimes and Punishments* Voltaire states that he read this little book with infinite satisfaction. Like medicine it could be compared to one of the few remedies that were capable of alleviating suffering and be a means of softening the remains of barbarism in the laws of many nations. Punishment, he said, was frequently worse than the crime and was sometimes detrimental to the state it was intended to serve. Ingenious punishments like the wheel, which was first introduced in Germany, and which endeavoured to render death horrible, seem rather the inventions of tyranny than justice. He also recorded a number of very harsh cases that exemplified what it was that Beccaria was intent on destroying.

At the time of the Inquisition Voltaire opposed the death penalty for heresy and sacrilege and argued for the utmost toleration for all religious sects. A Calvinist teacher who was detected preaching to his flock in certain provinces was put to death and those who gave him supper were sent to the galleys for life. In other countries a Jesuit caught preaching was hanged.

---

8. Cesare Beccaria. *An Essay on Crimes and Punishments with a Commentary by Monsieur de Voltaire.* pp. i – lxxix.

Were not these punishments to avenge God? Yet, it was our duty to honour the deity not revenge him.

In the year 1748, said Voltaire, at Wurtzburg in Germany an old woman was convicted of witchcraft and burnt at the stake. How incredible, he exclaimed, that a people who had boasted of their Reformation, and of having trampled superstition under foot, should believe in witchcraft. For an allegation of witchcraft which could not be proved, another woman was executed in Geneva after having confessed under severe torture to being an agent of the devil. At this period, he said, every tribunal in Europe resounded with such judgments and fire and faggot were universally employed against witches and heretics. When the Turks were reproached with having amongst them no witches, sorcerers or demons, this absence was considered to be infallible proof of the falsity of their religion.

In countries where a trifling domestic theft, or breach of trust, was punished with death, was not the disproportion of the punishment to the crime dangerous to society, asked Voltaire. The punishment being the same for a small theft as for a greater, he would naturally steal as much as he could and at last would not scruple to turn to murder to prevent detection.

Dealing with confiscation, Voltaire said that it was a maxim at the Bar that he who forfeited his life also forfeited his property. This, he continued, prevailed in those countries where custom served instead of law. Hence, the children of someone who committed suicide (then a crime) were condemned to perish with hunger equally with those of an assassin. In every such case a whole family was punished for the crime of an individual. In feudal times princes and lords, not being very rich, sought to increase their revenues by the condemnation of their subjects. But now their power was founded upon immense and certain revenues there could be no justification to swell their treasuries with the wrecks of unfortunate families.

Voltaire also dealt with the question of blasphemy. Lewis XI, King of France, who for his virtue was made a saint, made a law against blasphemers under which he condemned them to a new punishment; their tongues were pierced with a hot iron. It was a kind of retaliation with the sinning tongue suffering the punishment. But it was somewhat difficult to determine what was blasphemy. Expressions frequently escaped from a man in a passion, from joy, or even in conversation which were merely expletives without the least intention of swearing by God.

The words which are called oaths and blasphemy are commonly vague terms that may be variously interpreted. The law by which people are punished for such matters seems to be founded on the Jewish saying, "Thou shalt not take the name of the Lord thy God in vain". But the best commentators were of the opinion that this commandment related to perjury.

On criminal procedure, Voltaire complained that in France the legislators had been influenced by too much severity. In many instances criminal procedure pointed only to the destruction of the accused. It was the only law which was uniform throughout the whole country and which should certainly be no less favourable to the innocent than terrible to the guilty.

In France a trial was conducted in conditions of secrecy. A single judge heard each witness separately based upon a misreading of the Penal Code. The judge could easily influence what a witness might say and on his second examination, also in private, if the witness retracted from his earlier evidence in any material particular he could be punished for giving false evidence. A man suspected of a crime was denied counsel and was encouraged to flee abroad. Then he was condemned in his absence without a trial. The law denying counsel to a defendant was plainly unjust.

In England, he said, the criminal law was common to the whole country. In France, however, he deplored the fact that the criminal law varied from one region to another. He also followed Beccaria in dealing with other issues such as high treason, the death penalty, torture and suicide on which his views have been outlined earlier in this book.

PART 3:

BECCARIA'S INFLUENCE

CHAPTER 8

PROFOUND IMPACT

The French Revolution and Adversary Trial

Although Beccaria was inspired by the French Encyclopædists he also had a profound influence upon them. According to one magistrate, his book, "did much to transform the spirit of the French criminal courts even ten years before the Revolution; that all the younger magistrates of the courts (and he himself was one of them) pronounced their judgements in conformity with the principles enunciated in that work rather than in accordance with the existing laws..."[1] It might be said, he added, that *On Crimes and Punishments* had considerably hastened the approaching revolution in France.[2] Clearly, its enlightened and humane concept of jurisprudence complemented the work of the Encyclopædists in laying the intellectual groundwork for the destruction of the *ancien regime*.

Hence, one of the first reforms of the Constituent Assembly in 1789 was the preparation of a criminal code based upon the work of Beccaria, with more than one hundred offences ceasing to incur the death penalty, and the new English approach to adversary trial being accepted in place of inquisition, secrecy and torture. The *Declaration of the Rights of Man* of the same year proclaimed the presumption of innocence at precisely the time it was argued for in London's Old Bailey by the celebrated English advocate, William Garrow. A jury system, with grand and petty juries as in England, and with justices of the peace, was instituted in France and torture was abolished along with some of the powers of the public prosecutor.

Also abolished, in 1791, were branding and mutilations with a decree that the death penalty should consist only in the deprivation of life, not

---

1. Letter of magistrate Rœderer to Beccaria's daughter, Giulia, in May 1798. Cited in Coleman Phillipson. *Three Criminal Law Reformers: Beccaria, Bentham, Romilly*. New Jersey, Patterson Smith, p. 83.
2. Coleman Phillipson. *Ibid*.

accompanied by tortures such as the wheel. Then, in 1795 the Convention resolved that capital punishment would be totally abolished when peace was declared. In effect, almost all traces of inquisitorial procedure were swept away and replaced with a French copy of the system of English adversary trial. In England men's minds were becoming ready for a system that would deliver equality without erecting an all-powerful state that would at the same time destroy human rights. As Vogler has written:

> Bearing in mind the subsequent spread of adversariality around the globe, it is difficult to escape the conclusion that it bore some deeper relationship to the social, political and industrial changes then underway in England. It seems too much of a coincidence that the first industrial nation should also be the first to develop this mode of trial process and at the very same time. As has already been pointed out, the 'lawyerisation' of the trial was in many respects an opening of the feudal court hierarchy to the market and in that sense, just as much a "commercialisation". Moreover, the constitution of the defendant as a rights-bearing actor in the process cannot be unconnected with changes in the status of the individual in the new employment market.[3]

England was in the throes of rapid change and, in a sense, the political events that had given rise to the Glorious Revolution in opposition to royal power acted as a midwife in bringing into the world a new philosophy stressing the importance of the individual in society. The Whig hierarchy, which had recently suffered from arbitrary law, determined to introduce the right to a fair trial – at least on charges of treason.[4] They were not prepared, however, to extend that right to felony trials.

But there were other fundamental and far-reaching adjustments also taking place that would alter the cultural face of society world-wide. In particular, the Industrial Revolution, the growth of the market, the Enlightenment and the American and French Revolutions with their *Declarations of Rights,* each evoked powerful responses in bringing to light the importance of individual

---

3. Richard Vogler. (2005) *A World View of Criminal Justice.* Aldershot, Ashgate Publishing Limited, p 144.
4. A. H. Shapiro. (1993) "Political Theory and the Growth of Defensive Safeguards in Criminal Procedure. The Origin of the Treason Trials Act of 1696.' Illinois, 11(2) *Law and History Review.* American Society of Legal History.

human rights. In such circumstances adversariality, alongside the criminal jury and a presumption of innocence, became crucial components of the judicial system, a safeguard against abuse of power or maladministration by the state.

It was against this background that lawyers in England, of whom Garrow was foremost, consciously or unconsciously acted in a manner that fostered adversary trial, with barristers dominant, and its accompanying rights for prisoners. Indeed, such a form of trial extended process rights to all prisoners and

> the proposition that the Crown in a criminal prosecution was an adversary on equal terms with the humblest subject was startling and far-reaching in its application. The same lawyers who achieved this practical transformation from deference to debate went on to elevate the doctrine to a full-blown political ideology in the revolutionary creeds of the late 18th century.[5]

For the prisoner in the dock charged with felony and weighed down by rules and prejudices that, unless the jury showed mercy or he received a royal pardon, meant he was in serious danger of ending up on the gallows, the change to adversary trial was a total transformation. And it not only flourished in England but was widely and quickly adopted in other lands, including the United States, and it had a vital impact on criminal procedure around the globe.

These momentous upsurges in English national life, and the intellectual ferment they aroused foreshadowed human rights becoming an integral part of the legal, moral and political fabric of civilised society in which today the courts play "a leading role in resolving human rights controversies and developing human rights norms".[6] In this development of adversary trial Garrow played a critical and pre-eminent part which also enhanced the concept of due process of law. Whilst this was achieved by a practising lawyer, which Beccaria was not, Beccaria had earlier set out the philosophy which lay behind it. He had been born some 22 years before Garrow.

---

5. Richard Vogler. *A World View of Criminal Justice. Op. cit.* p. 131.
6. Steiner & Alston. (1996) *International Human Rights in Context: Law, Politics, Morals.* Oxford, Clarendon Press, pp. v-vi.

Human Rights and Voltaire's Causes Celebres

Prior to the publication of Beccaria's work, Voltaire had exposed unjust trials and atrocious treatment of prisoners in the repression of Protestant dissent and particularly with the sensational cases of Calas and Sirven. On 9 March 1762, Jean Calas was found guilty of having murdered his eldest son who was found hanged in the textile shop of Calas in Toulouse, allegedly in order to prevent his conversion to Catholicism. The murder enquiry was incompetently conducted by local magistrates who arranged an elaborate requiem mass for the son who had probably committed suicide. The following day, after suffering torture to make him identify accomplices, Calas, who insisted on his innocence throughout, was publicly broken on the wheel, strangled and burned by order of the French Parlement. Anti-Huguenot hysteria broke out in the local Catholic community with Protestants becoming fearful of leaving their homes.

Voltaire, who had spent some years in England where he had been deeply impressed by English criminal trial procedure, conducted a vigorous press campaign which had a widespread effect throughout Europe in convincing public opinion that the judges had allowed their anti-Huguenot prejudices to influence their verdict. As a consequence a panel of 50 judges reversed the conviction and awarded compensation of 30,000 livres.

Another of Voltaire's *causes celebres* was the case of Pierre-Paul Sirven. Protestant Sirven's mentally handicapped daughter, Elizabeth, disappeared on 6 March 1760, aged 21. It was later found that she had been taken into the convent of the *Dames Noires* under a *lettre de cachet*, which meant she had no trial or opportunity of appeal. As we have seen, *lettres de cachet* were the means by which many were able to send their opponents to the Bastille and other prisons and institutions for long term incarceration without trial. After Elizabeth's subsequent release following abuse, three children found her body down a well. A court sentence was passed on her family in their absence, condemning her father to be broken on the wheel, her mother to be hanged and her two sisters to be banished. It comes as no surprise to learn that the family fled and they found refuge in Lausanne where they contacted Voltaire. Over four years Voltaire campaigned for the Sirven family but all his efforts were rebuffed by the Royal Council. However, Sirven returned to France where the feeling over Voltaire's exposure of the Calas case aroused support for him and his family who were belatedly exonerated by the Toulouse Parlement.

As we have seen, Voltaire had a profound appreciation of Beccaria's work as is recognised in his *Commentary* added to the French translation of *On Crimes and Punishments* and his subsequent writings. In the *Commentary* he argued that reform of penal law was an absolute necessity. He cited a case where within a few miles of his home a girl of 18 was condemned and executed for abandoning her new-born baby. Away from her home she was taken in labour and without assistance was delivered of the baby by the side of a wood. She then left the child exposed and returned home, and the baby was found the next morning. Voltaire accepted that she was culpable, but because a child was dead, he cried in anguish over whether it was necessary to kill the mother. She did not kill the child and weakness had a right to indulgence. Where charity was wanting the law was always cruel.

Furthermore, she might, he wrote, have intended to return to the baby and provide for it – "a sentiment so natural in the breast of a mother, that it ought to be presumed". The law was unjust because it made no distinction between one who murders and one who abandons her infant. The law was inhuman because it punished with death a desire to conceal a weakness. The law was pernicious because it denied the state of a worthwhile citizen. The nation should provide houses of reception for exposed innocents. The purpose of jurisprudence was to hinder the commission of crimes, not condemn to death a weak woman without malice who had already been severely punished by "the pangs of her own heart."

Ensure, as far as possible, he wrote, a resource to those who are tempted to do evil and you will have less to punish.[7]

Like Beccaria, Voltaire opposed the violence of the French penal code in all its horror. As a consequence, on 30 May 1768 he wrote to Beccaria in praise of his stress on the importance of reason and humanity as against

---

7. Commentary by Voltaire to Beccaria's *Essay on Crimes and Punishments*. (1775) London, F. Newbery, pp. i-iv.

bigotry and fanaticism and his dealing a death-blow to cruelty – "the malignant hand-maiden to religion".[8]

Voltaire died on 30 May 1778 at 83 years of age. Because of his championing of victims of the Roman Catholic Church he was denied a Christian burial. However, his remains were taken to Paris in 1791 by order of the National Assembly and enshrined in the Panthéon where they remain to this day. It was estimated that about one million people attended the procession through Paris when his remains were returned to the city.

John Adams

If, declares Beccaria, I have no other merit than that of having first presented to my country, with a greater degree of evidence, of what other nations have written, and are beginning to practice, I shall consider myself fortunate.

> But if in maintaining the rights of men and of invincible truth, I should contribute to rescue from the spasms and agonies of death any unfortunate victim of tyranny or ignorance, both so equally fatal, the blessings and tears of a single innocent man in the transports of his joy would console me for the contempt of all mankind.[9]

It is interesting that John Adams, a founding father of the United States of America and its second President, used this passage in his defence of British soldiers in the Boston Massacre trial in 1770. As John Quincy Adams, his grandson and sixth President, was later to recall, "the electrical effect produced upon the jury and upon the immense and excited auditory, by the first sentence with which he opened his defense, which was [a] citation from the then recently published work of Beccaria."[10]

The so-called massacre arose from a number of youths snowballing a party of redcoats. Some soldiers, without orders, fired at the youths, killing

---

8. Coleman Phillipson. *Three Criminal Law Reformers: Beccaria, Bentham, Romilly.* Op. cit. p. 85.
9. J. A. Farrer. Introduction to *Crimes and Punishments including a new translation of Beccaria's Dei Deliit e Delle Pene.* Op. cit. pp. 120-121.
10. Charles Francis Adams. (1856) *The Works of John Adams, second President of the United States, with a life of the author, notes and illustrations.* Boston, Little, Brown, vol. ii, pp. 238-9.

three outright and wounding others, two of whom died later. Some of the men were put on trial but there was no conclusive evidence an order to fire had been given, or about who fired the shots, with the result that all were acquitted. The passage from Beccaria, spoken with passion by John Adams, may also have had a powerful effect on the jury. Clearly, Adams' grandson thought so.

CHAPTER 9

CONCLUSION

Success

In continental Europe in the eighteenth century the Roman-canon inquisitorial system dominated the criminal law. Unlike England where a jury determined guilt or innocence, the judge in a trial had such extensive powers that, to prevent oppression it was considered necessary to limit his authority. According to Stephan Landsman, he could convict a criminal defendant in only two circumstances. These were:

> when two eye witnesses were produced who had observed the gravamen of the crime, or when the defendant confessed. Circumstantial evidence was never sufficient in itself to warrant conviction. These evidentiary rules made it impossible to obtain convictions in many cases unless the defendant was willing to confess. Roman-canon process authorised the use of torture to extract the necessary confessions. Thus, torture became a tool of judicial inquiry and was used to generate the evidence upon which the defendant would be condemned.[1]

So the cure was a bad as the disease. And there remained no presumption of innocence, no rules of criminal evidence such as the hearsay rule which excluded second-hand evidence, and the witnesses were called by the proactive judge, not by the parties' own lawyers. It was this system at which Beccaria aimed his fire and in its place he provided a viable and humane alternative. As we have seen, under his influence the canon inquisitorial system was replaced by adversary trial in the French Revolution although it was to be largely restored by Napoleon in 1808. This inquisition system has been used by dictators the world over and denies the human rights of the individual. It was Beccaria, the unlikely patrician, who first systematically

---

1. S. Landsman. (1983) 'A Brief Survey of the Development of the Adversary System.' 44(1) *Ohio State Law Journal*. p. 724.

revealed both the horror of the evils practised in the criminal law across Europe and showed why they should be destroyed and replaced. It was all to be part of a new type of liberal society.

Other men before Beccaria had opposed legal torture but he was the first to reveal its absurdity and secure its abolition in one country after another. The same is true of the death penalty which was an integral part of the legal system of all countries before he wrote his "little book". After that explosive weapon was published enlightened rulers were prepared for the first time in history to accept voluntarily some of the changes that were occurring in society and it can truly be said that Beccaria was the right man in the right place at the right time.

According to Farrer, the most successful adoption of Beccaria's principles of punishment occurred in Tuscany, under the Grand Duke Leopold. When he ascended the throne robberies and murders were rife and unrestrained by the use of the gallows, the wheel and tortures. But Leopold, in 1786, resolved to avail himself of Beccaria's plan. He published a criminal code which proportioned punishments to crimes, abolished mutilation and torture, reduced the number of acts of treason, lessened confiscations of property, destroyed the right of asylum and abolished all capital punishments including for murder. The result was that Tuscany, from having been the land of the greatest and most numerous crimes, became the best ordered state in continental Europe. During the 20 succeeding years only five murders were committed in the region.

Before his death Beccaria saw torture almost entirely abolished in continental Europe alongside a tendency to adopt the other principles he had proclaimed. Probably no other man ever lived to witness so complete an adoption of his radical proposals in penal practice, or so thorough a transformation of the system he attacked in setting Europe ablaze. Even though the ideas of change were already in the air it was he who gave distinct expression to the longings vaguely felt by millions of men and women in many parts of the globe.[2]

Beccaria's name is closely linked with the concept of total abolition of the death penalty since, before him and in his time, others, like Montaigne,

---

2. *Ibid.* pp. 37-8.

who decried its severity still wished to retain it for murder and sometimes for other crimes. Only Beccaria stood out for abandoning it altogether as too severe and useless as a deterrent. In addition, he saw that it is judicial murder by the state and an irretrievable penalty which cannot be reversed if an executed person is subsequently found to have been wrongly convicted. Although mistakes occur today it happened more frequently in Beccaria's time when defence procedure in criminal trials was in its infancy. Cases of innocent people being hanged were by no means rare.

Of course, errors of justice cannot always be avoided. One curious example is to be found in the pages of *The Times* newspaper of 1 March 1880. A church organist near Kiev in the Ukraine murdered a farmer with a pistol in the sacristy and then, when he had prevented the priest from giving evidence against him by confessing the crime to him, denounced the priest as the killer. The priest protested his innocence but was sentenced to hard labour for life. When, twenty years later the organist confessed his guilt on his deathbed, and the priest's release was applied for, it was found that he had died in custody only a few months before.

In Britain the death penalty was abolished only after bitter campaigning for two centuries,[3] but the initial spark for that crusade was ignited by Beccaria. In the nineteenth century Lord John Russell conducted the campaign in the House of Commons but he was ably aided by the Criminal Law Commissioners who made perfectly plain, in their reports and draft Bills prepared for Russell, the debt to Beccaria. And it was in the House of Lords, where the peers were the most intransigent opponents of abolition, that the commissioners' reasoned arguments turned the tables.

Revolution

The eighteenth century was a century of momentous change in the western world. It saw the end of monarchs wielding absolute power and, in some cases as in America and France, the downfall of monarchy itself. The

---

3. For the full story see Brian P. Block and John Hostettler. (1997) *Hanging in the Balance: A History of the Abolition of Capital Punishment in Britain.* Winchester, Waterside Press.

Enlightenment blazed the path of change and the aristocracy, joined by a rising bourgeoisie, began to savour power in government. The same period saw the emergence of the market and new capitalists as the Agricultural Revolution and Industrial Revolution took hold. New attitudes came to the fore as deference began its long, slow decline. It is significant that it was at this time in history that England, America and France each produced a Bill of Rights.

Not surprisingly in this period of transformation new ideas spilled forth in regard to criminal law and procedure. And that commenced with the philosopher and reformer, Cesare Beccaria, followed by the lawyer and advocate, William Garrow, and the statesman, Thomas Jefferson. Two American Presidents, John Adams and Jefferson, read and used Beccaria's book and Jefferson endeavoured to introduce his theories into law alongside the jury system and the adversary trial system which was being introduced in England by its criminal lawyers led by Garrow.

England

However, Beccaria was faced with the terrifying consequences of the inquisitorial system of trial as set out in the preceding pages and perhaps that led him to overstate the picture in England. It is true that England had the inestimable advantages of the jury system as well as the lack of torture and secret trials. But the plight of prisoners (who were unconvicted defendants) was grim indeed. They languished in appalling plague-infested conditions in prison and when brought to court were not allowed counsel to represent them with the result that many were transported or sent to the gallows with no recognisable form of trial at all. They were often illiterate, disease ridden and overawed by the pageantry of the court and the judge so that they were speechless when their lives depended upon a vigorous defence. Rules of evidence hardly existed and the pre-modern trial was "brutally rapid".[4] For instance, 54 felons put to trial over four days at Surrey Assizes in 1751 were

---

4. Richard Vogler. (2005) *A World View of Criminal Justice.* Aldershot, Ashgate Publishing Ltd., p. 133.

given an average hearing time of somewhere near half an hour.[5] According to one contemporary:

> The rapidity with which the trials are despatched throws the prisoners into the utmost confusion. Fifty or sixty of them are kept in readiness in the dock under the court, to be brought up as they may be called for. These men, seeing their fellow prisoners return tried and found guilty in a minute or two ..., become so alarmed and nervous ... that ... they lose all command over themselves, and are then, to use their own language, taken up to be knocked down like bullocks, unheard. Full two thirds of the prisoners, on their return from their trials, cannot tell of anything which has passed in the court; not even, very frequently, whether they have been tried; and it is not, indeed, uncommon for a man to come back, after receiving his sentence on the day appointed for that purpose, saying, "It can't be me they mean; I have not been tried yet".[6]

The criminal court often resembled a public bar with the judge, jury and spectators all adding to the bear-garden atmosphere. In this respect the BBC television series at the end of 2009 entitled "Garrow's Law" depicted the scene with unswerving accuracy. Coiners, counterfeiters, pimps and thieves abounded whilst thief-takers took government blood money to send innocent men, women and children to the gallows or slavery in Van Diemen's Land. However, the influence of Beccaria resulted in the gradual reduction in the use of the death penalty. Garrow led the pressure from the lawyers, which secured the rules of criminal evidence such as the presumption of innocence and the hearsay rule. Those lawyers created a revolution in criminal law that augmented the birth and growth of the modern concept of human rights.

In the nineteenth century Beccaria was hailed by the Criminal Law Commissioners[7] and by Jeremy Bentham who inspired so much law reform in that century. In continental Europe, Emperors and high-ranking leaders of

---

5. J.M. Beattie. (1986) *Crime and the Courts in England 1660-1800.* Oxford, Clarendon Press, p. 378.
6. Thomas Wontner. (1833) *Old Bailey Experience: Criminal Jurisprudence and the Actual Working of our Penal Code of Laws.* London, pp. 59-60. Cited in John H. Langbein. (2003) *The Origins of Adversary Criminal Trial.* Oxford, Oxford University Press. p. 318.
7. For more on the Criminal Law Commissioners see John Hostettler (1992) *The Politics of Criminal Law: Reform in the Nineteenth Century.* Chichester, Barry Rose Law Publishers Limited.

both sexes vied with each other to introduce into their laws and procedures the reforms outlined with such vigour by the philosopher and legal reformer, Beccaria. And it all started, on the continent and in England, with Beccaria and his little book, *On Crimes and Punishments*.

Conclusion

In effect, the whole of *On Crimes and Punishments* translates into a passionate plea for a modern system of human rights in criminal law and procedure which we have by no means yet entirely achieved and which, in England in some respects, we are at risk of losing what we have. The high-level attacks on jury trial since jury selection was opened up to nearly all adult citizens on the electoral register and the increasing restrictions placed upon magistrates exercising their independence are examples of why eternal vigilance is required for their protection. The same applies with adversary trial, in regard to which that fearless and outspoken modern-day advocate Geoffrey Robertson QC has said:

> For all the grandiose descriptions that have been offered of the adversary system of trial, and for all the pomp and self-esteem that tends to affect its professional participants, it is the best method we have yet devised for giving the suckers an even break.[8]

In summary, the essence of Beccaria's philosophy of penal law is that the surest way to prevent crime is not by the severity or flexibility of the penalty, but by the certainty of punishment. He believed there should be a fixed code of laws, drawn up in the vernacular, free from obscurity, and made clear to the public at large. Otherwise citizens could not acquire a consciousness of personal security that was so essential to social life. Ignorance and uncertainty of punishments, he says, lend assistance to the eloquence of the passions. Every citizen should know when his acts are guilty or innocent.

---

8. Geoffrey Robertson. Q.C. (1998) *The Justice Game*. London, Chatto and Windus, p. 386.

To crown it all, we should treasure that wonderful sentence with which he concludes the book:

> In order that every punishment may not be an act of violence, committed by one man or by many against a single individual it ought to be above all things public, speedy, necessary, the least possible in the given circumstances, proportioned to its crime, dictated by the laws.[9]

---

9. J. A. Farrer. *Crimes and Punishments including a new translation of Beccaria's Dei Delitti e Delle Pene. Op. cit.* p. 251.

SELECT BIBLIOGRAPHY

Adams, Charles Francis. (1856) *The Works of John Adams, second President of the United States: with a life of the author, notes and illustrations. By John Adams' grandson.* vol. ii. Boston. Little, Brown.

Beattie, John. (1986) *Crime and the Courts in England 1660-1800.* Oxford, Clarendon Press.

Beccaria, Cesare. (1769 edn.) *An Essay on Crimes and Punishments,* Geneva.

    (1775) 4th edn. *An Essay on Crimes and Punishments with a Commentary Attributed to Monsieur De Voltaire. Translated from the French.* London, F. Newbery.

    (1958) *Opere.* (ed. Sergio Romagnoli) Florence. Sansoni, 2 vols.

    (1986) *Essay On Crimes and Punishments.* Translated by David Young. Indianapolis, Hackett Publishing Company.

Bellamy, Richard. (ed.) (1995) *Beccaria: On Crimes and Punishments and Other Writings.* Cambridge, Cambridge University Press.

Birks, T.R. (1874) *Modern Utilitarianism: or The systems of Paley, Bentham and Mill examined and compared.* London, Macmillan & Co.

Blackstone, Sir William. (1809) The *Commentaries on the Laws of England.* vol. vi. London, T. Cadell.

Block, Brian P. and Hostettler, John. (1997) *Hanging in the Balance: A History of the Abolition of Capital Punishment in Britain.* Winchester, Waterside Press.

Coke, Sir Edward. (1797) *Second Institute.* London, E. & R. Brooke.

Croly, Rev. George. (1841) *The Life and Times of His Late Majesty George the Fourth.* London, H. Colburn.

Damhouder. (1554) *Rerum Praxis Criminalum,* Antwerp, chapter xxxvi.

d'Entrèves, A.P. (1964) Introduction to Alessandro Manzoni's *The Column of Infamy:* Prefaced by Cesare Beccaria's *Of Crimes and Punishments,* London, Oxford University Press.

Devlin, Sir Patrick. (1966) *Trial by Jury.* London, Methuen & Co.

Eden, William. (1771) *Principles of Penal Law.* London, B. White and T. Cadell.

Esmein, A. (1914) *A History of Continental Criminal Procedure with Special Reference to France.* London, John Murray.

Farrer, James Anson. (1880) *Crimes and Punishments including a New Translation of Beccaria's "Dei Delitti e Delle Pene"*. London, Chatto and Windus.

Fielding, Henry. (1753) *A Proposal for Making an Effectual Provision for the Poor, and for amending their morals, and for rendering them useful members of the society*. Dublin, John Smith and Richard James.

(1966) *Financial Times*.

Fisher, G. (1997) "The Jury's Rise as Lie Detector". New Haven, 107 *Yale Law Journal*.

Goldsmith, Oliver. (1766) *The Vicar of Wakefield*. London, The Folio Society (1971 edn).

Hansard. House of Commons. [15] [31] col. 500.

Hay, Douglas. (1975) *Albion's Fatal Tree: Crime and Society in Eighteenth Century England*. London, Allen Lane, Penguin Books Ltd.

Holdsworth, Sir William. (1938) *A History of English Law*. London, Methuen & Co. Ltd., Sweet & Maxwell. vol. xi.

Hostettler, John. (1992) *The Politics of Criminal Law: Reform in the Nineteenth Century*. Chichester, Barry Rose Law Publishers Limited.

(1994) *The Politics of Punishment*. Chichester, Barry Rose Law Publishers

(2010) *Thomas Erskine and Trial by Jury*. Hook, Waterside Press.

(2005) *The Criminal Jury Old and New: Jury Power from Early Times to the Present Day*. Winchester, Waterside Press.(April 2005)

Trial by Ordeal Milton Keynes. *Legal Executive* Journal.

(2009) *A History of Criminal Justice in England and Wales*. Hampshire, Waterside Press.

(2009) *Sir William Garrow: His Life, Times and Fight for Justice*. Hampshire, Waterside Press.

Jardine, David. (1836) *A Reading on the Use of Torture in the Criminal Law of England prior to the Commonwealth*. Given at New Inn Hall, Michaelmas Term. Published as a book in 1837 and reprinted in the *Edinburgh Review* vol. 67. (April-July 1838)

Johnson, Samuel. *The Rambler*. No. 114.

Kaplow, Jeffry. (1972) *The Name of Kings: The Parisian Laboring Poor in the Eighteenth Century*. New York, Basic Books.

Landsman, S. (1983) 'A Brief Survey of the Development of the Adversary System.' 44(1) *Ohio State Law Journal*.

Langbein, John H. (2003) *The Origins of Adversary Criminal Trial.* Oxford, Oxford University Press.

Maestro, Marcello. (1973) *Cesare Beccaria and the Origins of Penal Reform.* Philadelphia, Temple University Press.

Manzoni, Alessandro. (1964 edn) *The Column of Infamy:* Prefaced by Cesare Beccaria's *Of Crimes and Punishments.* London, Oxford University Press.

May, Allyson N. (2003) *The Bar and the Old Bailey, 1750-1850.* Chapel Hill and London. *The University of North Carolina Press.*

Morellet, Abbé. (1823) *Mémoires.* Paris. French Library of Advocates.

Paolucci, Henry. (1963) *Beccaria, On Crimes and Punishments.* New Jersey, Prentice-Hall, Inc.

Paley, William. (1785 edn.) *Principles of Moral and Political Philosophy.* In *The Works of W. Paley.* (1825) vol, vi. Edinburgh, Peter Brown and T. & W, Nelson.

Parliamentary Papers. (1836) Criminal Law Commissioners Second Report. vol. xxxvi. (1837) Criminal Law Commissioners Third Report. vol. xxxi.

Peterson, Merrill D. (1970) *Thomas Jefferson & the new nation.* New York, Oxford University Press.

Phillipson, Coleman. (1970) *Three Criminal Law Reformers: Beccaria, Bentham Romilly.*

Montclair, New Jersey, Patterson Smith Reprint Series.

Radzinowicz, Sir Leon. (1948) *A History of English Criminal Law and its Administration from 1750. The Movement for Reform.* vol. i. London, Stevens & Sons Limited.

Robertson, Geoffrey. (1998) *The Justice Game.* London, Chatto and Windus.

Romilly, Sir Samuel. (1786) *Observations on a Late Publication, intitled, "Thoughts on Executive Justice".* London.

Shapiro, A.H. (1993) "Political Theory and the Growth of Defensive Safeguards in Criminal Procedure. The Origin of the Treason Trials Act, 1696". Illinois, 11(2) *Law and History Review,* American Society of Legal History.

Shapiro, B.J. (1983) *Probability and Certainty in Seventeenth-Century England. A Study of the Relationships Between Natural Science, Religion, History, Law and Literature.* New Jersey. Princeton University Press.

Steiner & Alston. (1996) *International Human Rights in Context: Law, Politics, Morals.* Oxford, Clarendon Press.

Stephen, J.F. (1883) *A History of the Criminal Law of England*. vols. i and ii. London, Macmillan.

   (1877) "Suggestions for Reform of the Criminal Law". *Nineteenth Century.* London, Sampson, Low & Marston & Co. *The London Magazine.* (July 1752) vol. 21.

Twining, Professor. (1973) "Bentham on Torture". *Northern Ireland Legal Quarterly.* No. 3, vol. 24.

Vogler, Richard. (2005) *A World View of Criminal Justice.* Aldershot, Ashgate Publishing Limited.

   (2006) *Criminal Justice and Due Process: A Global Revolution.* Unpublished Lecture in Lewes, Sussex.

Voltaire, François. (1775) *Commentary to Beccaria's On Crimes and Punishments.* London, F. Newbery.

   (1766) *Commentaries on Beccaria's 'On Crimes and Punishments' by an Avocat of Provence.*

Walpole, Horace. (1822) *Memoirs of the Last Ten Years of the Reign of George II.* vol. i. London, John Murray.

Wilde, Oscar. (1963 edn.) *The Soul of Man Under Socialism.* London, Spring Books.

Young, David. (1986) *Cesare Beccaria. On Crimes and Punishments.* Indianapolis, Hackett Publishing Company.

INDEX

A

abhorrence 54
absolute power 141
abuse 37, 113
　abuse of power 133
"Academy of Fists" 23, 30, 32
accomplice 39, 45, 102
accusation
　mere accusation ix
Adams, John 26, 136, 142
adultery 87, 88, 101
adversary trial x, 107, 116, 131, 139, 144
affirmation 95
Africa xii
Age of Enlightenment xi
aggravating circumstances 94
Agricultural Revolution 142
allegiance 79
America xi
　American Revolution 132
　Latin America xii
　North America xiv
　United States of America xiv, 26, 136
　modern use of torture by 49
Amnesty International 49
anarchy 54, 68, 73, 120
　anarchy on the throne of justice 106

anti-Huguenot hysteria 134
apathy 78
appeal 73
arbitrariness 29, 69, 84, 97, 132
aristocracy xvi, 30, 79, 112, 142
Aristotle 70
assassination 79
assumptions 87
asylum 140
atonement 111
atrocious crimes 99
attempt 102
Austria xi, xii, xv, 48
authoritarianism xii, 22
authority 72

B

banishment 134
bankruptcy 93
barbarity 27, 53, 54, 56, 72, 117
　excessive barbarity 120
　legalised barbarity 28
Bastille 134
battle 116
Beccaria, Cesare
　death of 33
　introverted xiii
　traits and origins 21
Bellamy, Richard 28
benevolence 26, 67
Bentham, Jeremy 28, 64, 69, 105, 143
Bergasse, Nicolas xi
bias 27, 105

bigotry 136
Bill of Rights
　Bill of Rights (USA) 26
　various 142
Birks, T R 64
Blackstone 51, 52, 60, 116
blasphemy 127
　tongue pierced with hot iron 127
　vague term 128
blood money 107, 115, 143
Bloody Code 46, 51, 68, 81
Boston Massacre 136
bourgeoisie 142
branding 27, 131
breach of trust 113, 127
breaking on the wheel 27, 51, 119
　example of (Calas) 134
Britain 79
British Aerospace case (jury power) 76
Brougham, Lord 65
brutality x
burden of proof ix
burning alive 51, 64
　burning at the stake 51, 127
Bush, George W xiv

C

Calas, Jean 134
Campbell, Sir John 65
canon law 91
capital crimes ix, xiii
capitalism
　growth of in England 27

Carolina (French) Penal Code 39
castration 51
Catherine the Great xv
Catholic Church 22, 39, 59, 136
censorship 84
certainty 118
chains 55, 86
challenging the status quo x
chaos 71
charity 77, 135
Charles II 80
China xiv, 49
church xii, 29
citizen 72, 123
  beast of burden 111
  good citizen 78
  war against 52
civilizing aspects ix
class 27, 112
clemency 124
close observation 123
Code d'Instruction Criminelle xii
Code Louis (1670) xi
codification 58
"Coffeehouse, The" 25
coining 64, 143
Coke, Sir Edward 42
cold-blooded atrocity xiii
commerce 94
common crimes 80
commoners 112
common law xii, 41, 112
common sense xv, 104
community
  community spirit 125
  service to the community 113
compassion 38, 48, 54, 117
compensation 84
competition 30
confession 39, 42, 84, 85, 87, 95, 139
  false 38
confidence 114, 115
confiscation 140
conjugal fidelity 89
Constituent Assembly (1789) 131
contradiction 44, 105, 115
  caused by the oath 95
convention 73, 97, 100
corporal punishment 111, 113, 114
corruption xiii, 37
  laws of 123
counterfeiting 143
courage 126
cowardice 103
credibility
  witnesses of 105
crime
  affecting individuals 78
  "Crimes Difficult to Prove" 87
  crimes tending to the destruction of society 78
  encouragement to crime 113
  first crime 119
  injury done to society test 76
  crime prevention 25, 58, 63, 68, 82, 119, 120, 144
criminal 78
  reasoning 55
criminal code xv, 58, 131
  Russia 32
Criminal Law Commissioners 64, 83, 141, 143
criminal procedure 116, 128
  irregularity of criminal procedure 28
cross-examination 107, 117
crucifixion 51
cruelty xiv, 28, 67, 74, 118, 136
  acts of wanton cruelty (crimes) 106
  consecrated cruelty 43
  cruel stupidity 106
custom x, 37, 39, 43, 48, 68, 77, 88, 91, 127

D

Damhouder of Bruges 38
darkness 122
"dead in law" 105
death penalty ix, xiv, xvi, 22, 25, 27, 51, 67, 107, 126, 131, 140
  irreparable 60
  lottery 62
debtors
  confinement of 68
decapitation 51
decency 51, 80
Declaration of the Rights of Man 131
defence x, xi, 24, 99, 142

Index 151

deference 142
depravity 121
despair 126
despotism 61, 69
deterrence 29, 53, 54, 70, 82, 118
  accomplices 102
  general and individual 82
Devlin, Patrick 75
Diderot, Denis x, 25
discretion 27, 41, 59, 73, 82, 94
  discretionary laws xvi
  unlimited discretion xiii
disease 142
disembowelling 51
disgrace 45, 87, 114
dislocation of bones 45
disorder 54, 74
disquiet 27
Disraeli, Benjamin 30
dissuading criminals 29
diversity
  of opinion 30
dogma 45
double jeopardy 100
Draconian Code of Athens 51
due process xiii, 133
duty 81

E

economics 30, 32
Eden, William (Lord Auckland) 61
efficiency 118
elites 30
Elizabeth I 42
eloquence
  power of 71
Encyclopaedists x, 25, 131
  French 30
England xi, 26, 28, 41, 60, 70, 79, 82, 95, 115, 116, 131
England's Bloody Code 46
English courts
  bear-garden atmosphere 143
  plight of prisoners in 142
  prison conditions 142
Enlightenment xiii, 122, 132, 142
enquiry
  time for enquiry 100
  ensuring the continued existence of society 82
entails 30
equality ix, 30, 81, 132
  equal penalties for unequal crimes 100
  inequality inevitable and useful 112
error 123, 141
Essay on Conscience (Montaigne) 38
ethics 73, 78
Europe 27, 28, 30, 37, 49, 51, 57, 70, 79, 87, 94, 105, 140
evidence 59, 85, 86, 87, 95, 103, 105, 115, 116, 139
  circumstantial evidence 139
fabricated evidence 107
false evidence 128
hearsay rule 143
rules of evidence 116
rules of evidence non-existent 142
rules of evidence (or no) 107
evil xiv, 26, 38, 55, 75, 103, 119, 120
evil intention (mens rea) 76
Ewart, William MP 65
example
  making an 62, 124
  exciting passion 83
execution
  wheel on 27
executive ix
expediency 102
extortion by minor officers of justice 68
extradition 96, 97
eye for an eye 29

F

fairness 75
  right to a fair trial 132
false divinities 122
false ideas 75
false imprisonment 117
family 33
  family spirit 125
  "the good of the family" 126
fanaticism 70, 79, 82, 114, 118, 136
fanatical sermons 83

Far East xii
fear ix, 62, 70, 90, 96, 112, 124
  fear of citizens 37
  fear of the law 121
felony 133
fetters and chains 55
feudal times 127
Fielding, Henry 60, 82
filth and horror of English prisons 68
fines 112
fire and faggot 127
Firmian (Count Firmian) 22
forfeiture 127
  estates 49
  property 127
forgery 92
Fox, Charles James xii
Fragment on Smells 28
France ix, xi, xv, 27, 28, 48, 117, 118, 128, 129
fraud 93, 113
Frederick II of Prussia xv
freedom 25, 29, 55, 69, 74, 126
French Revolution 59, 131, 132, 139
friendship 115
fury 70

G

galleys 126
gallows ix, 81, 107, 133, 140, 142, 143
  abolished in Russia 57

Garrow, William 107, 116, 131, 133, 142
general interest, the 124
generosity 117
Geneva 127
  Geneva Convention xiv
Germany 52, 126, 127
getting away with crime 120
Giannone 21
gibbet 55, 82
Giuseppe Grandi 34
Glorious Revolution 27, 112, 132
"golden book" 32
Goldsmith, Oliver 61
good 120
  good faith 93, 115
  goodness xi
  public good 125
goodwill 114
government
  weak government 37
gravity of the offence 60
great crimes 80
greed 124
growth of the market 132
guilt
  association by 45
  assumption of 99

H

habeas corpus xi
hanging 51, 59
  hanging, drawing and quartering 51
  hanging in chains 65

happiness 28, 29, 56, 58, 69, 74, 100, 115, 120, 124
home in 125
hardened soul of the criminal 55
hard labour 55, 141
harm 29
  preventing 70
  to society 53
harshness 97
  harsh punishments x
hatred
  universal hatred 97
heart of man 54, 72
Helvetius 24
heresy 126
Hippolytus of Marsailles 38
Hobbes 24
Holdsworth, Sir William 60, 116
homicide 100
homosexuality 87, 89, 101
honesty 93
honour 78, 91, 114
  public dishonour 114
hostile individuals 72
house arrest of Beccaria 22
humanity x, xiv, 21, 58, 63, 67, 77, 110, 135
  false humanity 99
  inhumanity 48
  offending humanity 97
human nature 97, 100, 120
human rights x, xiv, 97, 116, 132, 134, 144
human sacrifice 57
Hume 24
humiliation 112

hunger 127
hunting with a blackened face 51

I

ideology 81
ignorance 44, 77, 79, 122, 123, 136, 144
  ignorance of danger 84
illiteracy 142
ill-repute 114
immunity 87
impalement 51
imprisonment 83, 108, 113
  imprisonment without trial 102
impunity 97, 100, 120, 124
inconvenience xii, 74
indolence of the rich xiii
Industrial Revolution 132, 142
infamy 114
infanticide 87, 89
informers 37
inhuman actions 119
iniquity
  gradations of 61
injury done to society by crime 112
innocence 38, 40, 43, 63, 86, 87, 94, 104, 106, 115
  danger of condemning an innocent man 101
  presumption of innocence ix, 107, 116, 131, 133, 139, 143

inquisition
  Holy Office of the Inquisiition xii
  The Inquisition xv, 21, 33, 126
inquisitorial system ix, 37, 59, 132, 139, 142
insurance 75
intellectual stimulus xv
intention 76
  mere intention and attempt 102
interpretation 75, 77
intimidation 102
iron cage 55
Iscariot, Judas 91
Italy ix, xii, xv, 28, 32, 34, 107, 126

J

James I 96
Jefferson, Thomas 26, 142
Johnson, Dr 61
Joseph II 59
judge 27, 43, 44, 72, 73, 74, 106, 116
  as an advocate of the Crown 85
  as the enemy of the accused 86
  crime by 79
  ill humour 75
judges as prosecutors ix
judges should not assume the role of legislators 72
naturally on the side of authority 76

proactive 139
judgment of God 41
judicial
  judicial abuse 72
  judicial caprice 27
  judicial ferocity and cruelty ix
  judicial killing 55, 56, 141
judiciary
  lack of independence ix
jurisprudence 27, 33, 115, 131
  censorial jurisprudence 64
jurist 116
jury xii, 131, 133, 139, 142
  jury nullification 75
  modern-day attacks on 144
  refusing jurors 105
justice 52, 59, 79, 81, 126
  as a bond 72
  as an income generator 127
  divine justice 63
  injustice 30, 75, 124
  justice of the peace 131
  justice should be swift 27
  lack of 27
  vindictive justice 61

K

Kant, Immanuel 25
Kaunitz 59
kindred 115
King Hammaurabi of Babylon 51

knowledge 77, 121

L

land 30
Landsman, Stephen 139
law
  backed by force 90
  bad law 113
  good law 90
  guardian of the law 123
  ineffectual 90
  interpretation of 72
  law-based hereditary system 23
  laws of nature 88
  mild system of 124
  obscurity of 77
  pernicious 135
  purpose and need for 28, 53
  rigorous laws often produce crimes 113
  rigour of the criminal laws 62
  spirit of the law 74
  "temporary repairs" 115
  tenderness of the law 63
  useless laws 90
lawyer 106, 116
  hostile lawyer 116
  "lawyerisation" of trials 132
leading questions 94
legal representation for the defence 65
legislation 120
legislator 73
  judge as 99

views and errors of 78
leniency 118
Leopold, Grand Duke 58, 140
lese majesty 107
less serious crimes 100
lettres de cachet 134
Lewis XI, King of France 127
Lex Talionis 29
liberal despotism xiii
liberal society 140
liberty 29, 67, 78, 81, 111, 121
  deprivation of 54
Lieutenant of the Tower of London 42
life imprisonment 55
living society 72
Locke, John xv
logic 74
Lombardy xi, xii, 48, 59
  Supreme Economic Council 32
lying 121

M

Madan, Rev. Martin 62
magic art 111
magistrate 27, 37, 72, 73, 81, 84, 123, 131, 144
  Beccaria as 33
  enemy of the accused (France) 118
maladministration 133
martyrdom 96
mathematical calculations 44

morals of 29
May, Allyson N 116
medieval spirit 68
mens rea 76
mercy 24, 81, 124, 133
  God of mercy 78
Middle East xii
military virtues 30
miscarriage of justice 116
misery 120
  home in 125
mistake 83
moderate and continuing penalties 54
Montaigne, Michel de 38, 140
Montesquieu 23, 37, 42, 68, 72
morality 29, 53, 79, 103, 114, 115
  immorality 121
  Moral and Political Philosophy 63
  moral certainty 104
  moral sentiment 39
  political morality 70
  private morality 126
  public morality 126
motive 92, 100, 120
  religion and 96
murder 26, 42, 65, 111, 134, 140
  state murder ix
  Murder Act 1752 82
mutilation 27, 58, 131, 140

N

Napoleon

Napoleonic Code (Code Napoleon) xi
  restores inquisitorial system 139
national security 53
natural law 70
nature of man 86
Nemesis Theresiana 39
Newgate Prison 64
nobleman
  crimes by 81
  punishment 111
noise 83
Norman policy 51
nothing to lose 92

O

Oates, Titus 80
oath 95
  becomes gradually a mere formality 96
  vague term 128
obligation 73
obscurity
  language of 144
  of the law 77
offences
  income generators as 85
offensive prosecution 86
Official Secrets Act 1911 76
"Of the Treasury" 85
Old Bailey 107, 116, 131
  Old Bailey hacks 116
old-fashioned simplicity and honesty 77
On Crimes and Punishments x
open court 105
openness 145
oppression 67, 72, 123, 124, 139
ordeal
  see trial 41
ostracism 87

P

pageantry of the court 142
pain 38, 39, 40, 54, 55, 85, 95, 114
  least possible pain 83
Palatine School of Milan 32
Paley, Archdeacon 63
pardon 102
  by victim 124
  executive by 124
parental tyranny 23
Paris
  visit to 31
parricide 80
passion 84, 89, 128, 144
  stirring up hidden passions 115
patriot
  acting the patriot for others 63
peace 71, 83, 115
  justice of the peace 131
  king's peace 85
  peace of mind 37
peers
  trial by peers 105
peine forte et dure 42
penal code 57, 59
  France 128, 135
penal law x, 64, 69, 72, 106
penal reform 24
penal servitude 60
penance 42
Pennsylvania 59
people as objects 111
perfection 118
perjury 83, 107, 115, 128
philosophy 24, 30, 57, 69, 81, 86, 123, 132
  light of philosophy 122
Piazza Beccaria 33, 34
pillory 65
pimp 143
Plato x
pleas of the Crown 84
pleasures 28
police 115
political theories 27
pomp 123
Ponting, Clive 76
poor 30, 60, 111, 113
Portugal xi, 48
poverty 30, 60, 126
power 111
  ill-directed 28
  power of the state 69
precedent 106
prejudice 22, 64, 105, 133
preparatory acts 102
prescription 99
pressing to death 42
presumption 87, 88
  presumption 'in favour of' innocence 100
pretexts 45
principle 27
  "Principles of Penal Law" 61

Prisoners' Counsel Act 1836 65, 116
privilege 81, 111
  hereditary privilege 30
probability 104
  probability of a crime test 99
profit 85
proof 39, 40, 87, 95, 99
  acquittal for lack of proof 100
  discovery of proofs 99
  half-proofs 88, 101
  perfect and imperfect 104
  quasi-proofs 101
  Roman forms of proof 42
property 78, 90, 94, 111, 140
  offences against 61
proportionality 25, 29, 58, 70, 72, 100, 145
  disproportionality 113
  "Proportioning Crimes and Punishments in Cases Heretofore Capital" 26
prosecution 99
protection
  against harsh and oppressive laws 75
Protestant dissent 134
public
  public confidence 103
  public good 73, 90, 101
  public injury 81
  public policy 124
  public prosecutor (France) 131

public safety 58
public tranquility 83
punishment 26, 29, 48, 82
  certainty of 27, 97, 124, 144
  certainty of small punishment 119
  corporal punishment 81, 111, 113, 114
  degrees of intensity 54
  duration of 54
  effectiveness test 53
  efficiency 83, 118
  escaping punishment 119
  ingenious punishments 126
  lasting impression on the mind 118
  mild punishments 99, 118
  moderate penalties 69, 99
  need for restraint 71
  origins of 71
  prevention better than 120
  prompt punishment 82
  purpose of 58, 70, 82
  serious punishments 81
  severe punishment merited 111
  speed of punishment 99
  suitability of 68
  useless array of punishments 52
  worse than the crime 126
purging from sin 39

Q

Quakers 62

R

rack 38, 41, 42
Ramsay, Allan x
reason x, xi, 27, 28, 58, 64, 67, 74, 87, 135
  confused reasoning 64
reform 21, 24, 33, 61, 63, 68, 99, 144
  constitutional reform 25
  of the offender 26
  Reform Act 1832 65
Reformation 127
refuge 115
refusal to hear the grievances 123
religion 56, 71, 88, 95
  religious beliefs 29
  religious errors 122
  religious persecution 21
remorse 57
repentance 56
repressive laws xv
republicanism 125
repugnance 57
reputation 117
research 116
restitution 113
restorative justice 84
restraints of crime 99
retaliation 127
retribution 25, 29, 69
revenge 29
revolution x, 27, 53, 141, 143

reward 103, 115
rich 111
ridicule 114
right
　natural right 100
　social right 100
rights
　prisoners for 133
　right to life 71
　right to punish 71
riots 83
robbery 42, 61, 79, 112, 140
Robertson, Geoffrey QC 144
Roman law xii, xv, 29, 88, 91
Rome 117
　Roman magnanimity 117
Romilly, Sir Samuel 61, 62
royal
　royal despotism (in England) 112
　royal discrimination 112
　royal pardon 81, 133
　royal power 84, 132
　royal prerogative 112
rule of law ix, 54, 112
Russell, Lord John 65, 141
Russia ix, xi, 32, 48, 57, 110

S

sacrilege 126
safeguards 90
safety
　public safety 37
sanctuary 96
　petty sovereign state with 97

savage criminal procedures 25
Savanarola 83
Saxon dooms 84
science x, 77, 104, 121
secrecy 37, 59
　secret accusations ix, xiii, 21, 37
　secret trials 51
　　France, in 118
secular matters xv
security 69, 71, 80, 123
　lack of 37
　personal security 80, 100, 111, 144
　public security 124
　security of commerce 93
sedition 21, 80
seizure of goods 92
self-denial 30
self-love 124
sensitivity to human suffering 53
serious crimes xi, 85
Seven Years War 24
severity
　fear and 62
silence
　obstinate silence 95
　right to silence 95
sinning tongue 127
Sirven, Pierre-Paul 134
slavery 27, 43, 74, 80, 89, 121, 143
　creditors to 94
　family as a form of 125
　indefinite slavery 119
smuggling 91
social conditions 27

social contract xiv, 53, 69, 72, 77, 121
　violation of 113
social conventions 70
sovereign 74, 107
sovereignty 71
special
　special dispensations 27
　special interrogation 95
　special treatment
　　no place for 81
Spectator, The 25
spirit
　family spirit 125
　spirit of ferocity 53
　"Spirit of the Laws, The" 69
state
　in the interests of the state 76
　type and role 30
statute-barring 100
Statute of Treasons 1352 79
stealing a handkerchief ix
stealing a horse or a sheep 65
Stephen, Sir James Fitzjames 70, 76, 116
St. Petersburg 32
strangulation 134
Stuart and Tudor monarchs 41
subordination 126
suicide 53, 87, 90, 127, 134
superstition 127
Surrey Assizes 142
suspicion
　spreading 115
Sweden xv, 41, 48

T

taking the Lord's name in vain 128
tarring 51
temptation 60, 92
terror xi, 54, 55, 81, 82, 119
testimony 42
theft 111, 112, 127, 143
Theresa, Maria xii, 22
thief-takers 107, 115, 143
Thoughts on Executive Justice 62
tolerance 30
  human errors of 77
tooth for a tooth 29
torment 25, 29, 51, 70, 82, 83
  misery of torments 86
  useless torments 118
torture ix, xiii, xvi, 22, 27, 37, 58, 67, 87, 95, 101
  absurdity of 140
  during a trial 39
  excuses for torture 44
  gravity scale and 38
  mercy as 39
  modern-day use 49
  trial by torture 85
tradition 99
  diminishing of 77
transparency 145
transportation 60, 103, 107, 116
treachery 115, 121
  authorised treachery 103
treason 26, 42, 58, 65
  constructive treason 79, 80

high treason 51, 79, 80, 111
  reduction in types 140
trial 58
  incarceration without trial 134
  non-existent 39
  rapidity of (Surrey example) 143
  trial by boiling water 41
  trial by combat 41
  trial by fire 41
  trial by ordeal 41
trust
  distrust 115, 121
  mistrust 124
truth xv, 38, 41, 57, 68, 71, 86, 87, 101, 123, 136
  distinguishing from falsehood 44
  half-truth xv
  truth and error 122
Tudor and Stuart monarchs 41
Turkey 127
Tuscany xi, 58, 140
Twelve Tablets (Rome) 51
Tyburn xi
  monthly shambles at 61
tyranny 37, 38, 52, 53, 79, 111, 118, 126, 136
  exaggerating vice 90
  riches and 81
  unnecessary punishment of 48

U

Ukraine 141

uncertainty 74, 75, 77, 84, 103, 144
  as to fate 99
Utilitarianism 25, 28, 48, 69
utility 64, 69
  false ideas of 125
Utopia x

V

Van Diemen's Land 143
vanity 55
vengeance x, 69, 84
verdict
  jury verdict 76
  perverse verdict 75
  public verdict 105
Verri, Pietro 24, 31, 32
vice 71, 78, 90, 120
victim 84
  empathy xiv
vigilance 118
vigilante 84
violence 27, 48, 53, 55, 89, 90, 99, 111, 112, 135, 145
Virginia, USA 26
virtue 71, 78, 101, 115, 120
vision xii
Vogler, Richard 132
Voltaire xv, xvi, 25, 26, 30, 42, 48, 52, 80, 113, 117, 126, 134
  suicide, on 91

W

Walpole, Horace 61
war of human justice
 against iniquity
 117
waterboarding xiv
weakness 89, 124
 weakness has a right to
 indulgence 135
wealth 30, 111
wheel 52, 55, 119, 126, 132,
 140
 abolished in Russia 57
Whig hierarchy 132
whim ix, 27
wickedness 61, 100
Wilde, Oscar ix
Wilford, Thomas 82
Windham, William MP
 64
wisdom 63, 112
witchcraft 106, 127
wite 84
witness 105, 139
 credibility of witnesses
 105
 of ill-repute 106
women xvi
 as witnesses 105

Y

young people, youth, etc.
 23, 89, 131

www.ingramcontent.com/pod-product-compliance
Ingram Content Group UK Ltd.
Pitfield, Milton Keynes, MK11 3LW, UK
UKHW021329180426
11947UKWH00017B/1534